W9-BXV-883

The Negima Reader
Secrets Behind the Magic

cocoro books

Published by DH Publishing, Inc.
1-20-2-518 Higashi-Ikebukuro, Toshima-Ku
Tokyo 170-0013, Japan
http://www.dhp-online.com
cocoro books is an imprint of DH Publishing, Inc.

First Published 2008

Text and illustrations ©2008 by DH Publishing, Inc.

Printed in CHINA

Printed by Miyuki Inter-Media Hong Kong, Inc.
Compiled by Takeshi Abe and Adam Beltz
Publisher: Hirishi Yokoi
Design: Naohiko Sasaki
Editor: Yoichi Toyoshima
ISBN 978-1-932897-24-1
By courtesy of Akio Kurono (cac co,ltd.)

The Negima Reader: Secrets Behind the Magic

How to Use
In this book, the 13th in the popular Mysteries and Secrets Revealed! anime sourcebook series, you'll find everything you need to know about Negima and much more! And it's so easy to use. Just follow the Negima code below and within a few hours you'll be a Negima know-it-all.

Questions and Answers
Want to find out why who did what when and where? Then this is the book for you. There are 64 Q&As on every Negima topic, from school festival fights to Negi's training and tribulations.

Glossary
When you speak the lingo everything is so much easier. At the back of this book you'll find a comprehensive glossary of terms and names, explaining who's who and what's what.

Keyword Index
Want to go straight to Merdiana Magic Academy? Then start at the Keyword Index at the back of this book. There you'll find page links to every destination in the Negima world.

Negima Goods
Scattered throughout this book are fun Negima goods found only in Tokyo stores.

Summary

Introduction

Negima!: Master Negi Magi began publication in 2003 in Weekly Shonen Magazine and helped to sell over 10 million copies. When it was first released it was sold under the slogan "31 heroines for you to love" and appeared to be just another romantic comedy. But as the story progresses the reader slowly uncovers the true themes of courage and ambition as Negi continues on the search for his father, who is rumored to have died.

Aside from the comics, there have also been a variety of related books, CDs, games, and OVAs that followed. The anime aired on Japanese television in 2005 and 2007 along with a live-action TV show that is set to air in October of 2007.

Story Outline

Ten-year-old Negi Springfield is searching for his father, the legendary "Thousand Master," named as such because of his supposed mastery of 1000 spells. After graduating from his magic school in Wales, Negi moves to Japan to work as a teacher at the Mahora All Girls Secondary School and continue his training toward the goal of one day becoming a Master Wizard. He is the youngest teacher this class of 31 girls has ever seen, but before long various circumstances bring them all together and the search for the Thousand Master continues.

CONTENTS

The Negima Reader

The story opens with aspiring magician Negi Springfield at the graduation ceremony for the Merdiana Magic Academy. Negi, whose genius allowed him to skip two grades, was able to graduate just shy of his 10th birthday with only 7 years of study. At the ceremony, all graduates received diplomas with details on where they would go and what they would be doing for further training. Negi's diploma read that he was to become a teacher in Japan so, with that, he was off to start his new life.

As with many other schools, the diplomas at Merdiana Magic Academy require the president's signature before becoming valid, so it is nearly certain that Negi's going to Japan was the presidents will. The president of Merdiana and the school dean of Mahora Academy, Konoemon

Konoe, are also known to be old friends, further fueling speculation that the decision had been well thought out. The reason for Negi's going to Mahora is uncertain, but it may have something to do with his missing father, who had visited Mahora in the past.

There are many mysteries surrounding Negi's earlier years, but it's likely that the president had a reason for choosing distant Japan as Negi's training ground.

See Keyword

Negi Springfeld
Merdiana Magic Academy
Nagi Springfield
Konoemon Konoe

See Question
36

I n volume 1 of the manga, when Negi arrived at Mahora Academy he was greeted by an overwhelming number of students all clamoring to make it to class on time. While it may have been surprising to Negi at first, it's no wonder there are so many students considering that the school consists of K-12 and university in one unified campus. At roughly 100 years old, the school is well established and complete with its own railway and shopping district, making it a fully functioning city.

Some of the schools at the academy are:

The Mahora All-Girls Secondary School – The school where Negi teaches. This is a gender-segregated school where students go for grades 7-9. The seventh grade consists of 24 classes with a total of 737 enrolled students. Grades 8 and 9 are of a similar size, bringing the total number of students at the Secondary School to around 2200. The classes are fixed for the three years that students are there, with only the nameplate identifying the class number of each room changing. There are more than 160 clubs that deal in humanities, and another 21 that are dedicated to sports. Student dormitories are located on campus, but must be accessed by train as they are relatively far from school.

The Mahora Saint Ursula High School – A missionary school located next to the secondary school.

Mahora University – It would seem as though some of Negi's students' clubs have some kind of affiliation to the university: Satomi Nakase is in the Robotics and Jet Propulsion Clubs, Mana Tatsumiya is in the Biathlon Club, Lingshen Chao is in the Quantum Physics Club, Natsumi Murakami

See Keyword

Satomi Hakase
Mana Tatsumiya
Chao Lingshen
Natsumi Murakami
Zazie Rainyday

See Question
42

is in the Drama Club, and Zazie Rainyd is in the Magic Club.

Mahora University of Engineering

Mahora Fine Arts Middle School

Mahora International University and High School

Since Negi's living quarters hadn't been decided when he first arrived, the Mahora School Dean had requested that Asuna and his granddaughter, Konoka, let Negi stay with them. After that, Negi just simply continued living there. However, upon further consideration, it's a little strange for the dean to have suggested that as a solution in the first place. He surely would have heard of Negi's arrival from the president of Merdiana Academy, so why weren't arrangements made for him prior to his arrival?

It's most likely the case that when he made the decision the dean had known something about Asuna's latent powers; something of which she didn't even have knowledge. Similarly, Konoka had also been denied awareness of her family's magical background so that she could lead a normal life, but the dean may have figured that it was time for her to learn about her heritage. Therefore, Negi living with the girls was not just a spur-of-the-moment decision, but rather a well thought out plan to expose them to the world of magic and awaken their hidden abilities.

See Keyword

Asuna Kagurazaka
Konoka Konoe

04 Why does the clothing fly off of people every time Negi sneezes?

Negi graduated from the Merdiana Magic Academy with a specialization in wind-based magic. One of the spells that he learned was one that is supposed to strip his enemies of their weapons and clothing, leaving them both disarmed and humiliated. So, what really happens when Negi sneezes is that he looses control of his magic power and inadvertently releases this spell.

Naturally, this was a problem for Negi's victims, but he also suffered as a result of having to pay for all of the clothing he destroyed. This is especially problematic because he needs to help Asuna and Konoka pay for boarding so he simply can't afford to be paying for clothing all the time. To the dismay of many readers, he has gotten better at controlling his power though and it's been a while since he accidentally released this disarmament spell.

See Keyword
Disarmament Spell

05 What is a Magister Magi?

Negi went to Japan under the guise of a teacher for the Mahora Secondary School, but, one by one, people started to realize that there was more to this young boy than meets the eye. Asuna almost immediately became suspicious of Negi and confronted him on why he was in Japan, and it was at this point we learn about his goal of becoming a Magister Magi.

"Magister Magi" is Latin and loosely translates to "Master Wizard." The objective of a such a position is to help those in need and many end up working for a non-governmental organization. Magisiter Magi also have partners called Minister Magi, whose job is to serve as a sort of bodyguard and defend the Magister while casting spells.

Though many magic users work toward

this goal, there are relatively few who are able to attain the position and so far the Thousand Master is the only one who has been introduced in the story.

In Negi's case, he has been able to acquire quite a number of Minister Magi, but at the same time if too many people find out about the secret world of magic he may be turned into an ermine as punishment.

⑤ee Keyword

Nagi Springfield

From day one, the class representative Ayaka Yukihiro has showered Negi with an excessive amount of praise and attention.

The full-figured Ayaka is the second daughter and excels at academics and sports, making her seem much older than she really is. To fit her high-class stereotype, she is also an active member of the Tea Ceremony and Equestrian Clubs. Many people don't like her for her pompous nature but when she is around Negi she completely changes.

The reason for her becoming this way may have something to do with Ayaka's unborn younger brother. Everybody in the Yukihiro household was excited when her mother was pregnant with him and anxiously worked to prepare a room for him but their spirits were crushed with his miscarriage. Some people speculate that the affection that Ayaka felt for her brother were transferred over to the Negi, who happens to be the same age. This isn't the case for Kotaro, so it is likely she is attracted to Negi for his polite and caring demeanor.

See Keyword

Ayaka Yukihiro
Kotaro Inugami
Ayaka's Servants

Mahora Academy's 100-year history means that it has a lot of buildings. Of these is Library Island. Having the appearance of floating on water, Library Island is a massive structure that was used during World War II to house and protect books collected from various regions. When work was being done on the building, a huge labyrinth of books was discovered under the library. On the north side of this area there is an enormous bookshelf that extends over 320 feet high and at the very top is a waterfall that cascades down to the pool below. Aside from books, there are also fireproof doors and a wide assortment of treasures that are all heavily booby-trapped. With all the mystery surrounding Library Island and all the books waiting to be cataloged, something would have to be done to make sense of it all. To this end the Library Exploration Club was formed.

See Keyword

Yue Ayase
Haruna Saotome
Nodoka Miyazaki

See Question
08

21

In February of 2003, Negi began his work as a teacher in training and, in order for him to continue as a certified teacher when the new school year stated in April, he first had to pass a challenge given to him by the Mahora School Dean. His challenge was to improve his class's academic standing within the school.

At that point, even though Negi had a good number of intelligent students in his class, the class as a whole was still dead last in the school rankings. This was all thanks to none other than the Baka Rangers; an infamous group of fantastically underachieving students who were terrorizing the class score and keeping it from rising. In order for the class to do well on the upcoming final exams, and for Negi to keep his job, something would have to be done about this scourge of class 2-A.

It was rumored that a magical tome hidden somewhere in the library complex could raise the IQ of anybody who read it. Thus, a team lead by the Library Exploration Club was formed to retrieve this book in hopes of vanquishing the dreaded rangers and curing them of their stupidity once and for all.

Eventually, the group somehow manages to find the magical book only to fall through a trap door protecting it, and into the bowels of Library Island. Trapped inside the library with only three days before the exam, they gave up looking for the book and decided to settle in and study.

They barely made it back in time, but the studying paid off, and they were able to improve the class standing. And from April on, Negi became a full-fledged teacher.

See Keyword
Book of Melchizedek

See Question
07

09 Why did Evangeline attack Negi?

There are a lot of strange people in Negi's class, but the one with the strangest history is that of Evangeline A. K. McDowell. She may look like a harmless young girl, but she is actually a bloodthirsty Shinso vampire with a deep understanding of magic. In her earlier days she was feared by many and actively sought out Negi's father, Nagi, to suck his blood, which is how she ended up in Japan. But, instead of having the feast of her lifetime, she was tricked and trapped by Nagi in an anti-vampire soup of leeks and garlic. Being in a broth of her most hated vegetables, Evangeline was disgusted long enough for the Thousand Master to place a curse on her that kept her from leaving the Mahora Academy Campus, dooming her to a compulsory education in what he dubbed "Attendance Hell."

If Evangeline was to ever leave the

academy on her own volition, she would have to drink the blood of someone related to Nagi. So when she caught wind of Negi's coming to campus, she immediately began working on her plan of attack.

It was at around this time that we learn that the true reason Evangeline was chasing Nagi was that she developed strong feelings for him after he rescued her from falling off a cliff. Being the strongest vampire in the world, she doesn't have many friends and immediately warmed to Nagi when he treated her with kindness.

While she may have actually thought about using Negi's blood to free herself from her prison, in the end she ended up becoming friendly with him. She's stopped sucking the blood of random people but does drink Negi's on occasion, but not enough to cause any serious damage. It should also be pointed out that Negi's magical power is strong enough that it prevents him from becoming a vampire.

 See **Keyword**

Evangeline A. K. McDowell
Attendance Hell

 See Question
12

10 What is an activation key?

Before Negi casts a spell, he utters a Latin phrase that serves as his activation key. This key is a sort of password that mages use to unlock their true magical power. It is required for the vast majority of spells, but with a little practice some of the simpler spells can be used without activation keys. These are called chantless spells.

While still in magic school, students use a beginner activation key but are able to decide their own upon graduation. The key Negi chooses is "Tas Tel Ma Scir Magister."

11 Who made Evangeline's assistant Chachamaru?

From the antennas coming out of her head to the obvious knee and elbow joints, Chachamaru looks more like a robot than a human, but nobody in her class ever seems to mind. Mechanically speaking, she is a product of Chao Lingshen and Satomi Hakase, class 3-A's best and brightest minds. They collaborated on designing almost everything from Chachamaru's structure and AI to her rocket boosters and magic-canceling device. She has a socket in the back of her head in which a windup key can be inserted to power her, but this wasn't efficient and these days is powered by Evangeline's magic.

Evangeline uses Chachamaru as an assistant and is especially useful because, unlike her master, she is able to leave the school grounds to run errands. She does seem to have something of her own personality though and has become popular with people in town with her helping those in need and feeding of stray cats. Recently, she has also taken a liking to young Negi, but she hides this from her master.

See Keyword

Chachamaru Karakuri

N egi's class consists of people with different backgrounds, but one student with an exceptional past is Evangeline A.K. McDowell. She may look like an innocent young girl, but in actuality she is a centuries old vampire skilled in the ways of magic.

According to Evangeline's own account, she used to be nobility during the Hundred Years' War (1337-1453) between England and France. It's not known exactly how or why, but on her 10th birthday she was turned into a vampire and has been living as one ever since. That means that she must have been born somewhere between the years 1327 and 1443. So in 2003, when Negima! takes place, she could be anywhere between 560 and 676 years old.

Despite having the appearance of a cute 10-year-old girl, Evangeline's cold demeanor and unrelenting criticism of Negi hints that her 560 years of living has given her a great understanding of human values. Her mindset to never kill women or children shows that she still isn't an entirely evil person. Furthermore, she even feels bad for Negi when he's in a pinch and cries when she hears his life story. Her servant Chachamaru even said that Evangeline had calmed down since meeting Negi, showing that she may still have a human heart.

Evangeline is a vampire but she doesn't just go around sucking people's blood like she did in the past, instead opting to have some of Negi's on occasion. One might think that he'd turn into a vampire as well, but his strong magical power protects him from the curse.

See Keyword

Chacha Zero

Negi has a fair amount of book smarts, having graduated at the top of his class at Merdiana Academy, but when he had a confrontation with the battle-hardened Evangeline and her marionette servant, Chachamaru, it was clear that Negi was out of his league. There was still a fundamental element of Western Mages that the inexperienced Negi lacked.

When casting spells in battle, mages are vulnerable to attack, so it is common for them to make a special pact or, "pactio," with somebody who can protect them while fighting. A person who makes this kind of pact with a mage is called a Minister Magi and these contracts are typically sealed with a kiss after which the bodyguard's likeness is drawn onto a special card as proof of the contract. A kiss on any part of the face will seal the contract but it needs to be on the lips for it to be at full strength.

There are official contracts, but there are also provisional contracts, the type that Negi makes. There is no limit to the number of provisional contracts that can be made, allowing mages to search for the partner that he or she works with best. At this point in time, Negi has made provisional contracts with seven people.

A Western Mage's pactio bestows various powers onto his partner. Powered by the mage's magic, the Minister Magi's natural abilities are enhanced during battle, and further benefited by the use pactio cards. These cards can be invoked by the word "Adeat" which causes them to transform into special equipment or weapons called "artifacts." When finished fighting, uttering the word "Abeat" dismisses the artifact, causing the card to return to its original shape. The origin of these artifacts is unknown but it is speculated that, when summoned, they are on loan from the mages who crafted them.

The Magister and Minister Magi can also communicate telepathically with each other when separated. On top of this, the pactio card can also be used by a mage to summon his partner for battle, but since this involves interaction it may be difficult to pull off while actually engaged with the enemy. Teleportation only works one way with the mage being able to summon his/her partner; his partners cannot summon themselves to their master nor can they summon the mage to their location.

During the time Evangeline was trying to suck Negi's blood, he got a surprise visit from a spry little ermine named Albert Chamomile, or Chamo for short. This little guy wasn't just any ermine though, he could talk and identified himself as Cait Sith who was rescued from a trap by Negi and has kept in touch with him ever since.

He claimed to have come to Japan at the request of Nekane to watch over him, but the truth was that he was wanted by the police for stealing over 2,000 pairs of girls underwear.

Despite his lecherousness, Chamo is well versed in the ways of magic, and though he isn't much of a fighter himself, he is always able to give Negi good advice for how to deal with new foes. He was also the first one to tell Negi about the pactio system for making partners and was determined to get Negi to kiss as many girls as possible. While he did want to help Negi, he was also motivated by greed and wanted to collect the 50,000 Ermine Dollars commission per contract.

See Keyword

Albert Chamomile

16 Where is Negi's mother?

Negi came from Wales in search of his father, but no mention has ever been made of his mother so it's hard to know if she is even alive. It's also unknown whether or not he has any siblings. It's true that he does call Nekane "sister," and they do have the same last name, but she never calls Nagi "father" leaving us to assume that she is just a relative. The only other person that is known to have studied with Negi is Anya, and her full name is Anna Yurieuna Cocorowa so they are obviously not related either.

Negi is clearly determined to find his father, but it's truly a mystery as to why he never even so much as thinks about his mother. Could it be that there is some kind of magical spell locking these memories?

See Keyword

Nagi Springfield
Nekane Springfield
Anna Yurieuna Cocorowa

17 Why did Negi take his class to Kyoto?

Upon hearing from Evangeline that his father had visited Kyoto, Negi was eager to go there to see if he could find out more. He was afraid that he wouldn't be able to take time off work to travel but, as luck would have it, his class was scheduled to take its annual field trip around that time.

Having been the capital of Japan for nearly 1,100 years, Kyoto is historically and culturally rich and as such, many of its buildings and streets have been preserved. In this respect, it's a popular field trip destination so it didn't raise any suspicion when Negi chose it for their trip.

There was one more reason for Negi's going to Kyoto though. Konoemon Konoe, the Mohora Dean and member of the Kanto Magic association, wanted Negi to deliver a letter of peace to their conjuring Kansai counterpart. There had been a long stand-ing feud between the Kanto and Kansai Onmyodo Associations for quite some time and Konoemon felt that it was time to put the past behind them. The ever-enthusiastic Negi was happy to take the job, but had no idea of the troubles that would greet his arrival

It should also be pointed out that even though the Kanto and Kansai regions are relatively close, Negi's class lodged there for a total of five days and four nights. While this may seem like an overly abun-dant amount of time to some, an extended field trip like this is common practice in Japan as it gives students more time to relax and study.

See Question
19

Geographically speaking, Kanto is in the eastern part of Japan's largest island, Honshu, and Kansai is in the west. Japan's capital, Tokyo, is located in Kanto so some would consider it to be the cultural and political center of Japan. Many residents of the Kansai region disagree however, noting the area's richer historical background, with the ancient capitals Kyoto and Nara.

In the scope of Negima!, the Kanto Magic Association has taken the lead in pursuing ties with Western Magic and this has created tension with the more tradition-based Kansai Onmyodo Association.

However, the Kansai Onmyodo Association's way of thinking is outdated and inaccurate from a modern, global perspective. The magic of Western Mages isn't exactly free of tradition either seeing as the dead language, Latin, is used for chanting spells.

Chigusa is a perfect example of the kind of magic that the Kansai Onmyodo Association employs. This traditional Japanese form of magic is called "Onmyodou" and, instead of utilizing the partner system of Western Mages, it makes use of the Zenki, or "front demon," and Goki, the "rear demon." These demons are called "shikigami" and are actually nothing more than animated paper.

While some might think that the Kanto and Kansai Onmyodo Associations' different styles would compliment each other and make Japan a stronger magical power, in reality the differences only cause tension between the two groups.

See Keyword
Chigusa Amagasaki

See Question
19 20

K yoto is a world-renowned city for sightseeing but it's also a sacred city thought to be free of evil spirits. Around 1,200 years ago, the emperor killed his younger brother for his political opposition to the throne and, fearing divine retribution, decided to move his capital city to a more spiritually powerful location. This was the beginning of present day Kyoto.

The emperor decided his new city should be walled, but still be accessible from the North, South, East, and West by road with each entrance having its own gate named after a guardian spirit. This style of town planning was based on the Taoism idea of feng shui and is thought to have erected a massive barrier to evil spirits around the entire city of Kyoto.

The capital of Japan was moved to

Tokyo roughly 140 years ago so, naturally, the emperor moved to Tokyo as well. This kept Kyoto much as it looked in the past, and it still retains many of its historical buildings, streets, and even the ancient barrier that protects it. Therefore, it follows that the tradition-based Inyou Mages would choose a culturally and spiritually rich city like Kyoto for their headquarters.

Ⓢee Keyword

The Konoe Estate Shrine Maidens

Negi's class trip to Kyoto was plagued with problems from the very beginning. It all started when the letter of peace that Negi was to deliver to the Kansai Onmyodo Association was swiped by a shikigami swallow, continued with mysterious instances of frog and monkey infestations, and made a crescendo with Kanako's repeated abductions. This chain of events that lead to her kidnapping were the work of none other than the Kansai Onmyodo Association onmyou user, Chigusa. The intention of Konoko's captor was to control her with powerful drugs and magic and wield her great power to awaken a powerful demon and advance her own agenda.

Chigusa was nearly able to escape with an unconscious Konoka with help from her guarding demons, Enki and Yuki, but was thwarted at the last minute by Negi, Asuna, and Setsuna.

See Question 21

It's not known why the Chigusa would resort to such extreme measures to capture Konoka at this point in the story, but it is almost certainly related to the great war of the past. It would seem as though Chigusa suffered at the hand of Western Magic and has harboured a deep-rooted hatred for it ever since.

21 What exactly is Onmyou mages' Shikigami?

Chigusa used various types of shikigami to harass Negi when he was in Kyoto. Shikigami are spiritual beings that must do the bidding of their masters. They are initiated by writing a special incantation on a small strip of paper or plank of wood and can take different forms such as human, demon, or animal. Shikigami are capable of traveling great distances but revert to their source material if they or their master is defeated.

Onmyoudou has been handed down through the generations and has traditionally been used by the emperor or other high-ranking officials as fortune tellers, good luck, and protection from evil sprits.

See Keyword

Kishin, Usoku, and Kitsuneme

On the second night of their field trip in Kyoto, the students decide to spice things up by having a competition to see who can be the first to kiss Negi. The brainchildren of this competition were Kazumi Asakura, aka the Mahora Paparazzi, who was looking for the next big story, and the devious ermine Chamo, who wanted to increase the number of Negi's provisional contracts to collect money from the Pactio Committee.

The competition tuned out to be somewhat chaotic since so many of the students have secret crushes on Negi, but in the end it was the quiet, book-loving Nodoka who won. At this point, she didn't know that she had made a contract with Negi, but as the story progresses she learns of the great powers her pactio card holds.

Nodoka's artifact is a book named

Diarium Ejus. Upon uttering somebody's name in the book, it flips open to a special page that allows Nodoka to peer into his or her innermost thoughts. This is particularly useful in battle since she can use the book to glean important information such as an opponent's strategy or weakness. When Negi and his gang fell into a trap laid by the Kansai Onmyodo Association, Nodoka was able to use Diarium Ejus in this way to help them defeat Koutarou Inugami.

See Keyword

Nodoka Miyazaki
Kazumi Asakura
Kotaro Inugami

23 What are Kotaro Inugami's "Inugami"?

Kotaro's pointed ears, fangs, and long nails are all evidence of his unique Kuzoku origin. The word "Kuzoku" (狗族) roughly translates into "of the dog clan," so in other words Kotaro is half dog-demon and half human. Hired by Chisuga, Kotaro attacked Negi's group at the Genhiko Shrine as they attempted to deliver Konoemon's letter of peace to the Kansai Onmyodo Association.

The agile Kotaro is able to summon Inugami to attack and terrorize his enemies. According to Japanese lore, these spirits are said to be created by burying a living dog up to its neck in dirt and placing food just out of its reach. Days later, when the dog is on the verge of death from starvation, its head is to be severed from behind and buried under a busy crossroads to be tread upon. Finally, it is unearthed and enshrined.

And only then will an Inugami be born.

Kotaro's main style of fighting is to change into his true form and charge his enemy at full force while also making good use of the tormented Inugami. He can also channel "ki" to hurl Air Fang attacks.

See Keyword

Kotaro Inugami

S etsuna is a skilled user of the Kyoto Shinmei-ryu; a style of sword fighting developed in Kyoto specifically for the extermination of evil spirits. Traditionally speaking, disciples of the Shinmei-Ryu were charged with the protection of mages belonging to the Kansai Onmyodo Association.

Eishun Konoe, Konoka's father and leader of the Kansai Onmyodo Association, charged Setsuna with Konoka's protection but was only able to rescue Honoka from Chigusa with the help of Negi and Asuna. Later however, when the group is surrounded by a horde of demons and all hope seems to have been lost, Setsuna made a contract with Negi to become his third partner. Her newly acquired artifact is named Sicasinsicusiro; a short sword that can split into 16 identical swords that are controllable by mind. This deadly artifact makes Setsuna a true force to be reckoned with, allowing her to wreak havoc on enemies from every angle.

See Keyword

Setsuna Sakurazaki
Eishun Konoe
Tsukuyomi

Slapstick comedians in Japan sometimes use folding fans similar to Asuna's artifact, the Ensis Exorcizans. The fans they use aren't quite as powerful though since they are a simple composition of folded cardboard and tape. Despite this, if a comedian hits his partner on the head with one of these fans after he has made a mistake, it really seems to hurt. Anyway, the artifact that Asuna received after making a contract with Negi is a spoof on this idea as it is reflective of her strong yet clumsy nature.

The name Ensis Exorcizans translates into "sword of demon-banishing" and is quite effective as such, dropping demons with one deadly blow. The fan shaped Ensis Exorcizans isn't its true form however. When transformed, its power doubles as it takes the shape of a giant sword measuring slightly over 6 feet in length with a weight just shy of 9 pounds. At present, this form of the Ensis Exorcizans only emerges when Asuna is in trouble or when she looses control of her emotions.

S **ee Keyword**

Asuna Kagurazaka

Fate is the mysteries white-haired boy that helped Chigusa in her attempt to kidnap Konoka, but not much is known about him or his background. Even Konoka's father, the head of the Kansai Onmyodo Association, didn't have much information on the boy other than that he had arrived in Japan a month ago from the Istanbul Magic Association. Fate's excellent control of magic allowed him to single-handedly infiltrate the Kansai Onmyodo Association's headquarters and used a high-level petrifaction spell to turn nearly everyone to stone. His technique is so refined that not even Eishun himself could stop Fate.

Fate may not have much for emotion, but his knowledge of magic is abundant with fortes in stone and water magic. These spells include the area spell "Ishi no Ibuki"

(Breath of Stone), the petrifaction-based beam spell "Sekka no Jyakan" (Evil Eye of Petrifaction), the water-based entanglement spell "Suiyoujin" (Water Prison), and the ability to use water as a teleportation "gate." His style of magic seems to be mostly Western, but his charm-based spells such as Suiyoujin have a clear Eastern influence. It is entirely possible that he went to Japan with the intention of learning more about this unique type of magic.

When the fully powered Evangeline made her entrance, he was able to make a clean getaway, but Fate is destined to return.

See Keyword

Fate Averruncus
Breath of Stone
Evil Eye of Petrifaction
Stone Lance

Konoemon Konoe, the dean of Mahora Academy, holds the title of being the strongest on campus. As head of the Kanto Magic Association, it's obvious that he must be a quite capable mage, so why is it then that Konoemon didn't help out Negi and his crew after Konoka had been kidnapped? And wouldn't it have been faster and easier for him to go to Kyoto himself rather than sending Evangeline?

While Konoemon may be the strongest on campus, he knows that that is only because of the special barrier around the academy, which keeps Evangeline's power in check. If Evangeline were to leave campus however, her magical prowess would dwarf that of even Konoemon.

Another reason for his not helping may have to do with his being the chairman of the Kanto Magic Association. Interfering with the Kansai Onmyodo Association by squashing one of their rebel factions would likely create even more hostility toward the Western-friendly Kanto. In order to prevent groups sympathetic to Chigusa from popping up, Konoemon was better off sending Evangeline rather than getting directly involved.

See Keyword

Konoemon Konoe
Evangeline A. K. McDowell

28 Does the Ryomen Sukuna no Kami demon that Chigusa summoned really exist?

B
elieve it or not, there actually are accounts that colossal Ryomen Sukuna no Kami, whom Chigusa summoned with Konoka's power, really did exist. According to an ancient Japanese text called the "Nihon-shoki", nearly 1,600 years ago there was a two-faced demon with for arms and legs that terrorized the country and it took the dispatching of the government forces to finally quell the beast.

These days, copies of the Nihon-shoki are available to the public and the original is the second oldest historical document in Japan. In this day and age it might seem preposterous to think of some demon rampaging through the country, but in the days of the Nihon-shoki there was no doubt in the supernatural and it is not uncommon for this view to be reflected in historical texts. At any rate, there does appear to be some claim to Ryomen Sukuna no Kami's existence.

According to present-day scholars, the story of Ryomen Sukuna no Kami may have actually been inspired by two historical princes. These two were banished from the capital after having been suspected of plotting an uprising and were later crushed by government-led forces. Having been demonized by those in power, all that remains of these two princes is the story of Ryomen Sukuna no Kami.

See Keyword

Ryome Suku no Kami

Chigusa Amagasaki

29 Is Setsuna human?

During the fight in Kyoto between Chigusa and Fate, Setsuna was doing her best to rescue Konoka but as the situation became worse and worse, she become more and more desperate. It was at this time that she sprouted large white wings, finally revealing her true form and it was like this that she was able to finally come to Konoka's aid.

In reality, Setsuna is a half-demon, with her demon half being that of a Karasu Tengu; legendary creatures who look human but have beaks and dark black wings. Setsuna tried to keep this a secret from Konoka out of fear that she would come to hate her, but desperate times call for desperate measures and Setsuna was left with little choice.

 See Keyword

Setsuna Sakurazaki

M agic runs strong in Konoka's blood, with her father and grandfather being the heads of the Kansai and Kanto Magic Associations, respectively. However, she had no way of knowing this, let alone the fact that her magic abilities exceeded that of even Negi, since her father had brought her up to lead a normal life.

Chigusa had every intention of exploiting Konoka's latent powers to fulfill her own agenda, but was ultimately thwarted by Negi and his party. Having been wounded in this fight though, Negi was slowly falling victim to Fate's petrifaction spell. With his legs already turned to stone, Konoka had to act fast to save his life and formed a pactio with the unconscious Negi in order to do so.

Konoka has access to two artifacts;

the Japanese-style folding fans Flabellum Euri and Flabellum Australe. Neither one is designed for fighting but can instead be used for support. The Flabellum Euri can cure any physical wounds inflicted in the last three minutes, and the Flabellum Australe can cure all other ailments inflicted in the last 30 minutes.

See Keyword

Konoka Konoe
Konoemon Konoe
Eishun Konoe

Negi's Training and Tribulations

Negi approached Evangeline about becoming her apprentice the day after returning from the Kyoto fieldtrip. At first, she wasn't keen on the idea and had initially refused but eventually excepted, being moved by his strong dedication, ambition, and potential. But why would Negi dare to become the apprentice of a vampire like Evangeline, a natural enemy of the lawful mages?

During the fight with Chigusa in Kyoto, Negi put everything he had into defeating his adversaries. But despite his valiant effort, he simply wasn't strong enough to win. He was on the verge of death when Evangeline entered the scene and was able to decimate Chigusa's forces as well as the mighty Ryomen Sukuna no Kami, seemingly without effort. This display of absolute power was in sharp contrast with

Negi's helplessness, and it only served to amplify his realization of his own weakness. And with this it was decided, enemy or not, he would become Evangeline's apprentice to achieve his dream of being a powerful mage like his father. Besides, she had been his student before he even knew of her vampire origins and had not once even thought of her as being a bad person.

Another factor for Negi's decision was his partners Asuna and Setsuna. First and foremost they were his students and he figured that if he were stronger he wouldn't need their help, and thus they would never been in danger. This way of reasoning later got him in trouble with Asuna though, as she felt like she was an unwanted addition to his party.

Negi began taking Kenpo lessons from Ku Fei around the same time he became Evangeline's apprentice. As the head of the school's Chinese Martial Arts Club, Ku Fei is the strongest fighter on campus and is challenged to duals on a daily basis. He had witnessed her technique on one such occasion and immediately decided that it was something he wanted to learn. Even though Negi had high potential as a mage and had studied magic all his like, he still thought that also taking Kenpo would help to increase his overall combat ability.

When in Kyoto, Negi fought with the spirit wielding Kotaro and the white-haired Fate who are both capable of hand-to-hand fighting, and this put Negi at a disadvantage. He needed a way to defend himself and this is one of the main reasons he wanted to study Kenpo.

Negi's ambitious decision to learn both offensive magic from Evangeline and close quarter combat from Ku Fei is likely to prove to be a most effective combination.

ee Keyword

Ku Fei

See Question
33 34

33. What style of Kenpo does Ku Fei use?

It has been said that throughout China's history there have been anywhere between 400 and 600 different schools of Kenpo. Negi's instructor Ku Fei has specialized in the Keiken style of fighting but is also knowledgeable in the Hakkesho, Hakkyokuken and Shini Rokugouken styles.

The lack of flourish in the Keiken style is often equated with simplicity, but this is simply not the case. In reality, the simplicity in form is the result of hundreds of years of refinement. This style is one that stresses points such as posture and hitting technique to the utmost degree and is considered by many to be the most difficult forms of Kenpo to master. Many of the movements in Keiken mirror those of animals and it also incorporates the idea of defense and offense being one and the same.

Hakkesho has a number of different styles in of itself and tends to be much flashier than its straightforward Keiken counterpart. This style places emphasis on striking an opponent with the palm to deflect and block enemy attacks. At first glance, its light and flowing movements can seem more like a dance than a martial art, but it is said to be a form with limitless ways of striking.

Among all other forms, Hakkyokuken is the style that places the most emphasis on close quarters combat by making heavy use of the elbow-to-body strikes capable of defeating an enemy in one powerful blow.

The goal of Shini Rokugouken is to make the body and mind move in harmony by incorporating the movements of 10 animals such as the dragon, tiger, horse, monkey, snake, and bear. This secret style was originally developed by Muslims to protect themselves while traveling in China and though many people are now familiar with it, there are still some mysteries hidden in the form.

Ku Fei is only 14 years old but is at the level where she could be considered a Kenpo master. Where and how she learned it is unclear.

34 A What was Negi's Kenpo training like?

Evangeline required Negi to pass a test before she would allow him to become her apprentice. This test was to land even one blow on her servant Chachamaru without using offensive magic and relying only on his Kenpo training. This may have been easy if Negi's opponent had been a human, but Chachamaru is a robot that is armed to the teeth with high-tech weaponry and has been programmed for hand-to-hand combat. With such a formidable opponent and only two days to train, the test placed before him would require some special training from his master Ku Fei.

Negi's training got off to a rocky start with some questionable training that resembled something from an old Kung Fu movie, but Ku Fei quickly picked up on what areas her prodigy needed to improve.

At that time, even though Negi only had to land one hit to win the fight against Chachamaru, he was still no match for the robot, and even more so if the match were to drag on. So, Ku Fei considered two different strategies for victory; either catching the enemy off guard with a preemptive attack, or evading and countering an attack. With the fight being an organized match with rules, making a preemptive surprise attack was impossible, so it was decided that they would train in counter attacks. The dual nearly proved to be too much for Negi, but in the end he was able to take advantage of a hole in Chachamaru's defense when she became distracted. Having lost the bet, Evangeline kept her end of the bargain and agreed to take Negi as her apprentice.

See Keyword

Chachamaru Karakuri

Evangeline's training was rigorous, and aside from just magical training there was also hand-to-hand combat training that Negi partook with Chachamaru. Negi took the grueling training seriously though and was determined not to let her down.

The training took place inside her home and within a magical resort encased in glass. This resort is its own separate world where one day only equals one hour in the normal world, allowing for longer, more intense training. In this way, Negi was not only able to train under Evangeline's guidance, but was also able to continue his work as a teacher. While this may be an efficient use of time, there was still one question; why didn't Negi train together with his pactio partners Asuna, Nodoka, Setsuna, and Konoka?

The main reason is that, with the exception of Konoka's father having asked Evangeline to teacher her magic, nobody had even brought it up. Negi only had two objectives for the training; to become a powerful mage and to one day find his missing father. While Evangeline didn't voice particular interested in Negi's becoming all-powerful, finding his father was something that would serve her interests as well. However, after the trip to Kyoto, Negi had decided that he didn't want to endanger the lives of his students, and especially not for a personal reason like finding his long-lost father.

See Keyword

Evangeline's Resort
Nagi Springfield

36 Is Negi's father still alive?

According to official documentation, Nagi Springfield is by all accounts dead. If this were true, it would mean that he would have died before the birth of his son, Negi. However, Negi doesn't believe this to be true, claiming that the staff he currently uses is one that his father had personally handed down to him.

When he was younger, everybody told Negi that his father was dead and was never going to return, but at that time he didn't have a firm grasp on what exactly "death" was. All alone, Negi desperately wanted to meet his father and decided for himself that if he were in any great danger, his father would surely return to save him.

On a snowy day six years before the story takes place, Negi's home village was mercilessly attacked and destroyed by an angry horde of demons. And sure enough, right when all hope was lost, Nagi emerged from the shadows and effortlessly saved his son's life. It was after this confrontation that Negi received the staff from his father. However, assuming Negi's memory is right, the word his father used to describe the gift was "memento," and in Japanese a word like is only used to describe an item the deceased has left behind. If Nagi were truly alive, why would he choose to use such a powerful word?

It is true that during the attack on their village both Negi and Nekane were saved from petrifaction by somebody or something resembling the Thousand Master, but it's simply impossible to say with certainty that it was him in the flesh. In this world of magical intrigue, it's entirely possible that Negi may have been saved by his ghost from the afterworld, or perhaps he is alive but trapped in some alternate dimension. Whatever the case may be, the fact remains that the memory of this incident is the only one he holds of his father.

Upon meeting Albireo Imma, a previous partner of the Thousand Master, Negi was able to get close to confirming that his father is still living because of the active pactio card Albireo still holds, but even that still leaves some questions unanswered.

ee Keyword

Nagi Springfield
Nekane Springfield
Albireo Imma

After severely wounding Kotaro, Count Graf Wilhelm Josef Von Herrman then proceeded to ensure the capture of all the girls with a strong connection to Negi. One of Herrman's objectives was to gather information on Mahora Academy, Negi and Asuna, but there was another reason as well.

Herrman had been one of the demons that laid waste to Negi's home village and was responsible for turning many of the villages to stone. At that time, Negi was still a young child so Herrman wanted to see how powerful the boy had become since then. To this end he decided that the best way to gauge his true fighting ability was to make him angry by taking some hostages, and it worked. Making the boy angry was sure to pose more of a risk for himself, but he seemed to have had fun doing so anyway.

In truth, Herrman really doesn't seem like such a bad guy. He has a nice way of speaking, shows respect to his enemies, even let Negi know that there is hope for undoing the petrifaction which was cast on the villagers. In the end Negi was able to prevail over the demon, but didn't have the heart to finish his life. It may be a long shot, but with the almost friendly way that these two adversaries fought, could it be that Herrman might be somehow related to Negi and Nagi.

⑤ee Keyword

Wilhelm Josef Von Herrman
Kotaro Inugami
Ameko, Suramui, and Purin

The bottle that Herrman was trying to recover from Kotaro was the same one the old mage Stan used to seal him in during the fight over Negi's village. Naturally, he didn't want to be imprisoned inside the bottle for a second time, so its theft is what led him to chase Kotaro.

There are other mysteries surrounding Herrman and this bottle though. For starters, how was he able to escape from the bottle in the first place? Herrman is a high level demon, which means that the bottle must also be of superior strength. In other words, not just anybody can open this bottle; somebody with great magical know-how would have been required to break the imprisoning seal, allowing Herrman to escape. The goal of measuring Negi's power may not have been his own but the will of another.

Another issue that has yet to be addressed in the story is where the bottle was kept. Who was in change of the bottle? Where was it kept? Was it just left in the destroyed village? Surly somebody must have been looking after it, but who could that have been?

What ever the answers to these questions may be, it's likely that whoever it was that released the bottle had to first go through the work of stealing it with the intention of testing Negi's power by seeing if he could seal Herrman in the bottle once again.

⑤ee Keyword

Stan

Battles During the
School Festival

39 Exactly how big was the Mahora Academy's school festival?

Having completed the midterm exams, the students at Mahora Academy immediately set about preparing for the upcoming school festival that would see an amazing 400,000 visitors during the three-day period. Having come from a relatively peaceful school surrounded by natural beauty, Negi was surprised with the scale of the event but Yue nonchalantly explained that many of the visitors are from overseas.

To get a better understanding of the scope of the Mahora festival let's compare it to another popular attraction in Japan. The combined number of visitors to both Japan's Tokyo Disneyland and Sea parks is an estimated 67-68,000 people daily. So, in three days time, that would be 201,000-207,000 people, making the Mahora festival twice as big. It's hard to compare them when the Mahora festival only operates for three days out of the year, but it's still an extraordinary amount of people.

See Question 02

It's estimated that holding such an event would cost the school more than 2 million dollars per day to operate so the clubs that hold events during this day must make some money.

One of the most popular attractions during the school festival is a little restaurant called Chao Bao Zi managed by Chao with Satsuki as the chef. There is never an empty seat and it is quite capable of raking in a good amount of cash for a restaurant that is student run. The main reason for this is of course, the delicious food.

Satsuki actively participates in her school's cooking club and often brings samples of food to class for people to try. She always cooks to please and has no greater joy than seeing the faces of those who eat her dishes light up with satisfaction. As such, she decided from a very young age that it would be her goal in life to one day open her own restaurant. In a class of eccentric people, it is Satsuki's clear-cut and realistic goal that earns her respect from the Shinso vampire. Sure, there are other students who have clear goals, like Mana who works as a mercenary, but she leads a dangerous, unstable and desensitized life, making it impossible for her to be happy or to know what her future will bring.

Evangeline's own life was violently and irreversibly changed when she was only 10 years old, so she likely feels a bit of envy for somebody like Satsuki, who just wants to lead the simple life.

⑤ee Keyword

Satsuki Yotsuba
Chao Lingshen
Mana Tatsumiya

41 Why does the ghost of Sayo Aisaka haunt Mahora Academy?

The seat in the front row of class A closest to the window is haunted by a ghost. Sayo died in 1940 at the age of 15 and has wandered the halls and classrooms for over 60 years in search of happiness. It is thought that because of her shy disposition she was unable to make any friends before her death and remains in this world to do so.

Sayo's presence in this world is weak, making it difficult for most people to see her, including those with magical powers, and she was first noticed when her image showed up in a picture. This naturally caused a great deal of panic on campus and her spirit was nearly exorcised by Mana and Setsuna when Negi recognized her face from the class register and put a stop to their efforts.

In the end, Sayo was able to make

friends with Kazumi, who was able to see her having spent two years sitting next to her haunted seat. Even so, her sprit still remains in the school.

Ⓢee Keyword

Sayo Aisaka
Kazumi Asakura

42 Which clubs are Negi's students in?

During the school festival, many of the students in 3-A opted to make a haunted house for their class project. They nearly didn't finish it in time, but when all was said and done it was a popular attraction that was successful in terrifying all who visited. However, other students were responsible for helping with preparations as well. The breakdown of the clubs and those who are in them are as follows:

Chorus Club – Misa Kakizaki

Art Club – Asuna Kagurazaka

Manga Club – Haruna Saotome

School Newspaper – Kazumi Asakura

Library Exploration Club – Haruna Saotome, Yue Ayase, Nodoka Miyazaki

Tea Ceremony – Chachamaru Rakuso, Evangeline A. K. McDowell

Go Club - Chachamaru Rakuso, Evangeline

A. K. McDowell

Cooking Club – Chao Lingshen, Satsuki Yotsuba

Robotics Club – Chao Lingshen, Satomi Hakase

Chinese Medicine Club – Chao Lingshen

Bio-Engineering Club – Chao Lingshen

Quantum Physics Club (university club) – Chao Lingshen

Jet Propulsion Club (university club) – Satomi Hakase

Drama Club – Natsumi Murakami

Equestrian Club – Ayaka Yukihiro

Flower Arrangement Club – Ayaka Yukihiro

Basketball Club – Yuna Akashi

Soccer Club – Ako Izumi

Swimming Club – Akira Okochi

Track and Field – Misora Kasuga

Kendo Club – Setsuna Sakurazaki

Rhythmic Gymnastics – Makie Sasaki

Lacrosse Club – Sakurako Shiina

Biathalon – Mana Tatsumiya

Chinese Martial Arts – Chao Lingshen, Ku Fei

 ee Keyword

Natsumi Murakami
Yuna Akashi
Professor Akashi
Ako Izumi
Akira Okouchi
Misora Kasuga
Makie Sasaki
Makie Sasaki
Madoka Kugimiya
Sakurako Shiina
Zazie Rainyday
Fuka Narutaki
Fumika Narutaki
Kaede Nagase

 See Question
02

Cheerleading – Sakurako Shina, Misa Kakizaki, Madoka Kugimiya
Magic Club – Zazie Rainyday
Walking Club – Fumika Narutaki, Fuka Narutaki, Kaede Nagase

43 Why does Asuna like Takamichi so much?

While Asuna may act a little brazen and violent in front of her fellow classmates, she acted like a proper lady when Takamichi was the teacher of the class. Takamichi appears to be a perfect match for the type of guy Asuna likes; he is broadminded, kind, independent, and even a little rough around the edges, but much remains a mystery when it comes to this mysterious man.

When Asuna first came to the academy, Takamichi was the one who was in charge of looking after her, so it's no wonder that she developed a strong attachment to him. However, their history goes back even farther than that, to a time that not even she remembers.

As the story of Negima! progresses we learn that Asuna and Takamichi had met even before she joined the Mahora Academy as they both used to travel together alongside the Thousand Master. Another member of the group was one Gateau Vanderburg, who was the one that trained Takamichi in the art of fighting. Asuna never did seem to care for the man but couldn't hold back her tears when he was heavily wounded in battle and on the verge of death. Gateaus's dying wish was that Takamichi look after the girl and requested that she be freed of the memories surrounding this traumatic event.

While she may be inexplicably drawn to the sloppy, cigarette-smoking Takamichi, the image she sees in this man is actually just a reflection of his former teacher.

See Keyword

Takamichi T. Takahata
Gateau Vanderburg

See Question
52

I n the center of the Mahora campus stands a magical tree that is a massive 820-feet tall, more than twice the size of the Statue of Liberty. This tree, called the World Tree, is a well-known symbol of the Mahora Academy and the parks and restaurants surrounding it are popular locations. Aside from being a hang-out spot, it is also rumored that if one were to confess feelings of love to another under this tree on the last day of the school festival, there would be no chance of rejection.

According to Konoemon, this legend isn't just a thing of fantasy, but an actual occurrence that happens once every 22 years and is due to a massive building up of wood-based magical essence. When this has happened there are six different locations in which high concentrations of magical energy will enhance feelings of love and make any confession an instant success. While some may think this is a good thing, Konoemon disagrees saying that it is an abuse of magic to forcibly change one's emotions and this is the reason that the teachers were ordered to stop this from happening.

See Question 61

C hao has an intelligence far beyond most people her age. Not only does she always get the best scores on tests, but she also participates in the Cooking, Chinese Martial Arts, Chinese Medicine, Bio-Engineering, Quantum Physics, and Robotics Clubs.

She seems to be a perfect student but, truth is, Chao is actually somebody from one hundred years in the future with the goal of drastically altering history by making the existence of the magic well known to the world. This is of course a grave offence that would forever change the peaceful coexistence of magic users and the magic-less masses, and it is Chao's blind determination to do so that forced the teachers to chase her with the intention of erasing her memory. She was nearly detained by some of the school's magic-using teachers but Negi happened to be around and was able to save her from incarceration.

See Question 44 53

Negi was talked into joining the Mahora Martial Arts Tournament by the persuasiveness and persistence of Kotaro. It is said that this tournament used to be a grand event capable of drawing skilled fighters from around the world but became a mere shadow of its former self some 20 years ago.

This year however, the tournament was returned to its former glory with Chao's backing and the inclusion of a generous reward of 10 million yen, more than $80,000 for the winner. This spurred immediate interest in the tournament and drew a large group of 160 fighters.

While Chao insisted that the reason for this revival was simply to identify the strongest fighter, there was sure to be an ulterior motive. The rules for the tournament were simple: no firearms, no blades, and no chanting. The use of cameras and other recording equipment was prohibited to encourage magic users to join in for fun. Like clockwork, the magic users took the bait and soon even the teachers were signing up for the fight. Negi put his heart into the fight, having been spurred by the news that his father had been the last to win the tournament during its glory days. Everybody in the crowd seemed to be getting into the fight, but what they didn't know was that Chao's sinister plot was just beginning to unravel.

See Keyword

Pochi Digouin
Kaoru Goutokuji
Tsuji
Keichi Yamashita
Tatsuya Nakamura
Takane D. Goodman
Mei Sakura

47 What kind of ring did Negi get from Evangeline?

When training for the tournament at Evangeline's resort, she gave Negi a special ring with an incantation carved into it, which would allow him to invoke magic without the need of his staff.

When spells are cast, magical energy is drawn from the spiritual energy of the mage's surroundings and items such as the staff or ring assist in this process. Of course, the staff Negi received from his father is just as good as the ring at changing energy but Evangeline figured that the ring would be better suited to his newly developed Kenpo skills. The fight with Takamichi was the first time he used the ring, but coincidentally he also had a ring on his left hand.

See Question
35

48 Who has Misora formed a pact with?

Negi's student Misora seems normal enough in class but is a totally different person after the bell rings. In her free time, she likes to study as a nun under the guidance of Sister Shakti and is gifted with the use of magic. Misora would prefer to keep her ability secret but was found out by Asuna when she was pushed into using her magic while looking for Takamichi.

Misora's pact is with Cocone, an elementary student at the Mahora Academy, who is able to hear even the faintest of noises. Her artifact is a pair of sneakers that allow her to run at superhuman speeds and she mainly uses them to escape from hopeless battles.

See Keyword

Misora Kasuga
Sister Shakti
Cocone

Kaede is a talented ninja whose wide array of skills allowed her to proceed to the semifinals in the Mahora Martial Arts Tournament. The style that she trains in is the way of the Koga ninja, which along with Iga, makes up one of the two major forms. The main duties of ninja are to collect information on targets and to carry out assassinations. The Koga clan learned how to adapt to a changing world and incorporated the use of gunpowder in their techniques. In addition to this, they are also skilled in the area of medicine. Unlike the Iga, who acted more like mercenaries and would take any job if the price was right, the Koga were a loyal lot who served only one master.

On weekends, Kaede trains hard in the mountains surrounding the campus where she continues to hone her ninja skills. One technique that Kaede is particularly fond of is the where she splits herself up into multiple copies of herself to confuse and overwhelm her foes. It is a powerful attack that was even able to make the mighty Ku: Nel Sanders worried. Kaede is also skilled in the use of Shuriken and uses a giant cross-shaped one that is as intimidating as it is deadly.

See Keyword

Kaede Nagase

See Question
50

The man who proceeded to the finals by defeating both the half-demon Kotaro and the ninja Kaede was none other than the great Ku: Nel Sanders. He calls himself a librarian, but in the past he was a member of the Crimson Wing and is really a mage of outstanding ability. Ku:Nel Sanders is actually a magical clone standing in for Albireo Imma who is currently residing deep inside Library Island. While still a member of the Crimson Wing, he made a contract with the Thousand Master and still holds the resulting pactio card. The design on the back of Albireo's pactio card has never changed, meaning that it is still active, giving hope that Negi's father is still alive.

His artifact is called To Fyuron To Biographicon and it allows him to become a perfect clone of his opponents for up to 10 minutes, taking their appearance, physical abilities, emotions, personal preferences, and even memories. With this ability, he was able to take Nagi's form and advised Negi to stop trying to find him and instead focus on being himself. Negi was taken aback by what he had said, but understood what his father meant and decided that it was his own destiny to follow in his footsteps after all. Albireo seems to be an old acquaintance of Evangeline and is thought to have feelings for her since he teases her from time to time.

See Keyword
Albireo Imma

See Question
51

51 ✡ What is the Crimson Wing?

During the great magic war twenty years ago, Nagi worked for the NGO Austro-africus Aeternalls which was part of the UN. He worked closely with Eishun, Gateau, Albireo, and two others to form a band of six called the Crimson Wing. They were regarded as heroes of the war and are well known even today but the details of their exploits are yet to be revealed in the story. In his youth, Takamichi also tagged along with the Crimson Wing but was not an official member.

See Keyword

The Crimson Wing Forces
Nagi Springfield
Eishun Konoe
Albireo Imma
Gateau Vanderburg
Big Sword Man

Negi took over teaching at the Mahora Secondary School after Takamichi, who now holds a different position on campus as a supervisor. He is also occasionally sent on business trips overseas so he doesn't often come in contact with Negi. The truth is that he is still affiliated with the NGO group Austroafricus Aeternalls and often needs to help them with different jobs. Takamichi isn't a Magister Magi but he is still considered as an elite in the magical world with an AA+ ranking and has even appeared on the cover of magazines as such.

Takamichi was born without the ability to use incantations and hated himself for it, often saying that he is "leftovers of the magic users." He made up for this disadvantage by focusing his training on hand to hand combat and his efforts obviously paid off. He fought against Negi, and we could see some of his true powers, but many believe that he threw the match.

He often thinks about his time with the Crimson Wings and his guidance under Gateau. From him, he learned how to quickly attack his opponents without it even seeming as if he even moved. It is said that he visited Negi in Wales while he was very young and gave a display of his power by cleaving a 300-foot dragon in half using only his fists. He has high expectations for Negi but is still undecided as to whether or not he should tell Asuna about her past.

⑤ee Keyword

Takamichi T. Takahata
Gateau Vanderburg

During the school festival, Chao worked diligently in the background crafting and perfecting her master plan to reveal the existence of magic to the world. She had invested a lot of time into this project and she spared no expense keeping it secret, which is why she decided to keep the teachers busy with the Martial Arts Tournament. The phases in Chao's plan are as follows:

1. Conceal the reasons behind her choosing this period in time to return to, though it is possibly because of the incredible power Negi and Evangeline both posess.

2. Infiltrate the Mahora Academy at a young age and quickly make friends with the brilliant Satomi so that she has an ally and is involved in the creation of Chachamaru.

3. Start middle school as a Chinese foreign exchange student in 2001.

4. Enter the Robotics and Quantum Physics Clubs and use future technology to create high quality robots and use Chachamaru to hack the school mainframe during the blackout. (2001 – 2003)

5. Use the vast magic energy stored in the World Tree during the school festival to continue her plan. (June 2003)

6. Give the pocket watch time machine to Negi to let him experience time travel.

7. Use the Martial Arts Tournament as backdrop to reveal the existence of magic, but her plans were hindered by Chisame and teachers.

8. To win Negi over to her side. Was again foiled, this time by Setsuna and Kaede.

9. With the World Tree exposed, Chao returns to the future leaving behind a note that says she returned to her

hometown.

10. To change history with her actions. She was stopped and in the end the world knew of magic, and Negi was restrained.

11. To turn Negi away, but he came back to save Asuna so she used the remaining power of the World Tree to summon her Cassiopeia.

12. To collect energy from the six locations around the World Tree.

See Keyword

Chao Lingshen
Chisame Hasegawa

Yue is in the Library Exploration Club along with Nodoka and Haruka. She has admitted to having feelings for Negi and has support from her two friends even though Nodoka has already made her own feelings for him known. When this all came out on the second day of the school festival, Nodoka was taken aback but said that she would "cheer her on as a friend." Later that day, Yue made a contract with Negi.

Her set artifact is called Orbis Sensualium Pictus and consists of a cloak, book, witch's hat and broom. As it turns out, her set is the same as what students in magic school receive when they first begin their studies. The book is able to answer any questions related to magic. Additionally, it is connected to Maho Net and is therefore capable of auto updating itself, but because of this she is unable to access older records.

ee Keyword

Yue Ayase
Taizo Ayase
Nodoka Miyazaki
Haruna Saotome

See Question
07 42 60

The manga loving Haruna doesn't have particularly strong feelings for Negi but wanted to try forming a pact with him out of curiosity. Her artifact is called the Imperium Graphices, which is a set consisting a sketchbook, inkwell, quill, hat, and apron. When a picture is drawn in the sketchbook it will come to life, allowing her to control it. At first it may not seem like a good tool for combat but with a little innovation Haruna was even able to prevail in the fight against Chachamaru with a little help from Ku Fei. However, as summons, her drawings have no effect against people like Asuna, who have magic canceling abilities.

See Keyword

Haruna Saotome
The Sword Goddess

Simply put Chao gave Negi the small pocket watch named Cassiopeia in hopes of winning him over to her side. During the school festival Negi was hopelessly overbooked and needed to find some way that he could get to all of his appointments on time, and this is where the watch helped. With it he could go through the first day of the festival and use the watch to return to the beginning of the day so that he could make other appointments.

Why would Chao want to give such a powerful tool to Negi though? Could it be that she really wanted somebody to stop her? On the other hand there is also the possibility that changing the future would erase her, so maybe, in the bottom of her heart, she had hoped somebody would interfere, which is why she gave him the Cassiopeia. Of course, she would have continued with her plan of changing the future, but at the same time she may have given the watch to Negi with the idea of 'whatever happens, happens.' Or perhaps it is simply the case that Chao slipped up. It didn't even occur to her that she was enabling Negi to foil her plan. Whatever the case may be, it is certain that Chao had wanted Negi to have the Cassiopeia.

See Keyword

Chao Lingshen

See Question
57

N egi and Chao both use a small time machine called Cassiopeia and, while they may vary slightly, they are basically the same. Cassiopeia runs off magical power, meaning that more magical power is required the farther back one wants to move in time. It would be very difficult to try to use the clock consecutively to travel and, according to the user's manual, it is limited to a 24-hour time frame. This just raises the question that if even magic users can't travel back more than a day, how was it that the magic-less Chao was able to travel back 100 years? Could it be that she was somehow able to utilize the power of a large group of magic users? If that were the case she would need 365 mages to move back one year in time and 36,500 to move back 100.

Time travel can raise a great number of inconsistencies. For example, let's say we have a guy named Ethan. If for some reason Ethan was to travel to a time before his birth and killed his parents, there is no way he could ever be born. However, if he had never been born then there wouldn't have been any way he could have traveled back in time to kill his parents in the first place. This is what is commonly referred to as a time paradox.

Therefore, if Chao also were to travel back in time and cause a great disturbance of some sort, wouldn't that create a time paradox too? Sure she isn't exactly going back and killing her parents directly but there must be a risk that her very existence would be threatened. With Chao's plan, the history of the entire world would change and there is a chance that her parents never would have even met. If Chao hadn't been born though, history wouldn't have changed and therefore the world would still be oblivious to the existence of magic.

While there is a chance of creating a time paradox, the possibility of it occurring would have surely been something that the genius would have thought about. Knowing Chao would have put a considerable amount of planning into how she would change the past and what the results of that change would be so as to minimize the risk of erasing her own existence. Either she plans to succeed in creating a future where she is never born and simply continues living in some parallel world, or Chao's intention was to change history but in a way that ensures his existence. It's hard to say at this point what she is planning.

Chisame has a cold personality and has great disdain for the people around her who she views as bumbling airheads. Even after witnessing magic first hand at the Martial Arts Tournament, she still refused to admit that magic exists, but eventually caved in to the reality of the situation and became one of Negi's partners.

Her artifact is a scepter by the name of Sceptrum Virtuale and it allows her to enter a magical cyberspace with the assistance of seven electronic spirits that she can communicate with even in the real world. In addition to herself, Chisame can also enter cyberspace with people around her but their physical bodies are left behind in a trance-like state. Her seven spirits are usually controlled with their own software programs, but she also has the option of writing her own for more flexibility and did so to protect the school system from a cyber attack.

See Keyword

Chisame Hasegawa
Seven Electronic Spirits

See Question
60

60 △ Why is there magic-computer-based magic?

Chisame is an expert with computers and is also able to hack into Maho Net using her artifact. However, with computers being cutting-edge technology and magic being an ancient art, why has this craft been created? In the past, magic always existed outside of the realm of science, but with the dawning of the computer age all this changed and it was necessary for magicians to get with the times.

Aside from combat, Chamo also likes to use Chisame's artifact to connect to Maho Net for information gathering and online shopping. Other examples of magic and technology working together are Cassiopeia and the barrier that is used to keep Evangeline on the school's campus.

See Question
54 57

61 Why isn't the powerful World Tree better known?

The massive 820-foot-tall World Tree is a symbol of Mahora Academy and is one of the great magical hotspots in the world. Being larger than California's famous redwood trees and nearly as tall as a skyscraper, why is it that the World Tree isn't more famous than it is? With so many new students witnessing the giant tree firsthand each year, it's strange that word hasn't gotten out about it yet.

See Question 44

Thinking about the great power this tree harnesses, we can get an idea of why this is the case. People do in fact talk about the tree, but just like the magic that hides Negi when he is flying through the sky, the World Tree is also likely to have its own protective barrier.

62 About how many magic users are there around the world?

According to Chao, there are about 67 million magic users worldwide. The global population in 2003 was roughly 6.3 billion, which means a little over 1% of the world consists of magic users. One out of every hundred people may not seem like a lot, but it really is. The population of Tokyo is somewhere around 12 million, so that means the number of magic users in the world is more than five times that number and is only a little under the population of the entire state of California.

At dawn of the final day of the school festival, the students and teachers at Mahora Academy were able to thin out Chao's robot forces and victory seemed at hand when Mana appeared and started picking them off with her sniper rifle one by one. She had worked with the people at Mahora Academy during the field trip to Kyoto and again when they needed to stop confessions of love from being made under the world tree, so why did she suddenly turn against them? It surly must have something to do with her dark and complicated past.

In her past, Mana used to be a Minister Magi for a powerful mage and together wandered the earth carrying out missions for an NGO. Sadly, her master didn't survive the dangerous work and that left a deep impression on her personality and to this day she maintains a cold and indifferent person.

Chao's goal is to change the chaotic future by changing the past. Mana, who knows what it's like to live in a land of strife, may have been sympathetic to her cause and wanted to do her part toward making a better future. Mana herself even put this into words by voicing approval for Chao's actions and saying that she was only following her own conviction.

See Keyword

Mana Tatsumiya
T-ANK- 3 aka Tanaka

64 Chao isn't a magic user, so why does she use fire magic?

With the World Tree at maximum power, Chao was getting ready to carry out the final stage of her plan when Negi spotted her on top of a plane floating 4,000 meters above ground. Using a combination of his Cassiopeia and magical spirits, Negi was able to defeat Chao and foil her plans for a second time, but then surprised everyone by using the high-level fire spell "Blazing Heat in the Sky." Chao usually isn't able to use magic but was able to unlock her innate magic ability by using future technology. This came at a price though and even making the incantation for the spell lead to excruciating pain.

S ee Keyword

Blazing Heat in the Sky

Glossary

Character Profiles

The Teachers of Mahora Academy

Even though the story takes place in a school, the characters in Negima! come from a seemingly endless variety of backgrounds. Aside from the unlikely mishmash of students in Negi's class, there are also Western and Japanese Mages, robots, a ninja, dragon, and even a golem.

The purpose of this chapter is to offer greater insight into the personalities, abilities, and histories of this unique blend of characters.

The Teachers of the All Girls Mahora Secondary School

There are two types of teachers at the Mahora Academy: the teachers who use magic, and those who don't. At first glance, it might seem strange that the chairman of the academy is also the chairman of the Kanto Magic association but, as the story progresses, it's evident that the magic-wielding ability doesn't just end with him though. The reason behind the large congregation of magic users in one place can't just be a coincidence; it must have something to do with the massive World Tree that graces the school grounds.

Those Teachers Who Use Magic:

Negi Springfield

As an aspiring Master Wizard and the protagonist of this story, the Welsh Negi Springfield graduated two years early and at the top of his class from the Merdiana Magic Academy. He went to Japan to continue his training by succeeding Takamichi T. Takahata as the homeroom and English teacher for Mahora Secondary School's quirky class 2-A, which later became 3-A at the start of the 2003 school year. It seems he may also teach English to classes outside of his regular class as well.

Having inherited great magical ability from his father, the legendary Thousand Master, Negi has honed his skills through both formal and informal training to become a truly respectable adversary. His hardworking and straightforward personality makes him a true gentleman and he always comes through when times are tough but, being a kid, he is also known to be somewhat naive and obtrusive at times.

Negi is currently rooming in the girl's dormitory with Asuna Kagurazaka and Konoka Konoe.

Takamichi T. Takahata

Takamichi is a long-time acquaintance of Negi and was the previous homeroom teacher of Mahora Secondary School's 2-A class. He is rumored to have been classmates with Evangeline at one time and is said to have been able to easily quell troublemakers, earning him the nickname "Death Glasses Takahata"

He is most recognizable by his trademark glasses, stubble and heavy cigarette smoking. Asuna has begged him since childhood to quit, but that hasn't seemed to slow him down. His smoke of choice is Marlboro, and it is said that he owns a Dodge Viper.

Misora has also made allusions to his being the next dean of the Mahora Academy after Konoemon Konoe retires.

Konoemon Konoe

Konoemon is the grandfather of Konoka Konoe and current dean of the Mahora Academy. He is the most powerful magic user on campus and, as such, he also has powerful friends such as the head of Merdiana Magic Academy and is an old friend of Negi's father, Nagi. Konoemon has taken charge of Negi for the time being since his father is missing and thought to be dead. He sports a ponytail-like topknot at the end of his abnormally long head and wears western-style clothes.

In his free time Konoemon enjoys playing "Go" with Evangeline and they occasionally share a drink together as well. He also keeps himself busy arranging meetings between Konoka and prospective grooms, but one wonders why he bothers since she always seems to run away anyway.

Whenever a problem arises he typically leaves it up to the more capable youths, but isn't afraid to take responsibility if they happen to fail.

Seruhiko

Seruhiko is another one of the male, magic-using teachers at the Mahora Secondary School. He specializes in defensive magic and has said himself that he isn't particularly talented with combat.

Gandolfini

Gandolfini is part of the teaching staff but his actual department and position is unknown. Like Takamichi, the dark-skinned Gandolfini also wears glasses, but his style of fighting, with a pistol in his right hand and a knife in his left, makes him unique. He is rarely seen using magic, but this may be due to his preference for combat-based fighting.

Gandolfini is one of the more normal teachers, having an ordinary wife, and a daughter at elementary school, but he is one of the most obstinate as well, illustrated by his refusal to believe Negi about the time travel incident during the school festival arc. Later, when Gandolfini realized it was true, he lamented the fact that Negi's formally bright future had been ruined.

Mitsuru Nijyuin

Another one of the magic-using teachers of Mahora academy. Like Gandolfini, Mitsuru's department is unknown. Mitsuru is a stout man with narrow eyes but, surprisingly, is married with a kindergarten-aged daughter. His daughter can also use magic and utilizes dolls to conjure illusionary beasts. At first glance, Mitsuru seems to be a rather pleasant man but at the same time he also demands respect from those younger than him.

Professor Akashi

He is the father of Yuna Akashi and professor at the Mahora University. He helped Megumi to run the main computer at the festival during the Mages vs. Mars battle. He spends much of his time doing research and has helped to uncover more details on the backgrounds of Fate, Wilhelm, and Chao. Yuna is unaware of the existence of magic. Some say that she is also a little too attached to her father for being in Secondary School because she sometimes makes references to marrying him. Yuna's mother died when she was very young and her father has since become somewhat rough around the edges. This may be the reason for his daughter feeling as though she needs to support him.

Touko Kuzunoha

Touko's flowing blond hair

and voluptuous figure make her popular with the men. Normally cool and composed, at times she can also succumb to bouts of uncontrollable rage. Touko moved to the Kanto region after marrying a Western Mage in 1995, but later divorced and is back on the hunt. She was able to find a new boyfriend but, after Chao revealed the existence of magic to the world, there was a chance that she would be turned into an ermine and have to break up with him.

She invokes the power of a pactio card, which means that she must have made a contract with a Mage other than Negi.

Sister Shakti

The dark-skinned nun, Sister Shakti, acts as a role model and mentor for Misora and Kokone. She was attacked by Mana on her way to the Mahora Arena but was able to hold her own with her cross-shaped weapons.

Kataragi

Kataragi is one of the cooler teachers, with his slick-black hair, mostache, and sunglasses. Like Negi, he also specializes in wind-type magic and is able to use the Karmai Touch spell simply by snapping his fingers. He can also summon powerful tornadoes capable of encaging foes, and offers support from the backlines with spells for jobs where snapping just isn't enough.

Teachers Who Don't Use Magic

Shizuna Minamoto

She was the English teacher for class 2-A when Negi arrived in Japan. Since she hates cigarette smoke and is often seeing trying to get the heavy-smoking Takamichi to quit. It's not known whether or not she can use magic.

Nitta

His being the Director of Academy External Activities and strict zero-tolerance policies have earned him the nickname "Nitta the Ogre." He also teaches classes on Modern Japanese.

Ninomiya

Having studied Physical Education at university, Ninomiya now teaches at the Mahora Secondary School and also helps out with the rhythmic gymnastics club.

Negi's Students

Negi was assigned as a student teacher to class 2-A at the All-Girls Mahora Secondary School to continue his training. This rambunctious class of 31 is known for its pranks and had a few surprises ready for Negi when he walked into the room on his first day. While there were some students who didn't find this funny, most of the students broke into laughter at the inaugural prank.

This class can be a little hard for new teachers to cope with, but after getting to know them it's easy to see that the class is comprised of a surprising number of colorful and interesting students.

Asuna Kagurazaka

As the heroine of the story, Asuna has a bright, friendly, and thoughtful personality, but can be short-fused at times and is never afraid to speak her mind.

She prefers rough-cut, middle-age men and fosters a great discontent for irresponsible young kids. While Negi is technically a kid, he is tolerable only because he takes responsibility for his actions and, like Asuna, always tries his best at whatever he does.

Asuna moved to Japan seven years before enrolling at the Mahora Academy and upon entering the school immediately took a liking to the rugged Takamichi. On the second day of the school festival she was finally able to muster the courage to confess her love for him, only to be met with rejection.

With no parents to speak of, Asuna delivers papers in the morning in order to pay for her tuition and board. She dorms with her close friend Konoka and was later joined by Negi, who took up residency with them after his first day. At first, she despised the idea of living with a kid like him, but one thing led to another and before she knew it they had sealed a pactio with a kiss, making her Negi's first partner. Many people in her class think that they are dating, but Asuna really just feels a strong urge to protect Negi as a partner.

On the class trip to Kyoto, she was able to become close friends with Setsuna and eventually came to take kendo lessons from her to enhance her skill with the magic-canceling Ensis Exorcizans. She is rather talented when it comes to athletics and is a natural in combat, but she should try hitting the books for a change as her horrendous grades place her dead last in the class. This is exemplified by her membership in the "Baka Rangers" as "Baka Red."

Konoka Konoe

The quite and gentle Konoka hails from Kyoto and is the granddaughter of Mahora Academy's school dean, Konoemon. Being from Kyoto, she is somewhat traditional in that she enjoys doing housework and is always putting the needs of others before her own. She is also interested in fortune telling.

Konoka dorms with Asuna and Negi, whom she sees as a younger brother. She is also a good friend with Yue, Nodoka, and Haruna from the Library Exploration Club.

Konoka had been childhood friends with the sword-swinging prodigy Setsuna but their friendship seemed to have abruptly ended: Setsuna had been charged with Konoka's protection, but fearing Konoka would learn of her true origins, she preferred to watch over her from the shadows. After the incident on the Kyoto fieldtrip, Setsuna hit it off with Asuna and now usually tags along with her and Konoka.

Konoka inherited great magical power from Eishun, her father and head of the Kansai Magic Association, but he had hoped to keep it a secret from her so she could lead a normal life. Konoka was destined to awaken her true powers however, and there is a possibility that one day her magical prowess may develop to the point where she is utterly unrivaled in the realm of magic.

After the incident in Kyoto, Konoka made a contract with Negi to become his fourth partner.

Ayaka Yukihiro

Ayaka is the second daughter of Zaibatsu Yukihiro and is the A class's representative. She has a high-horsed opinion of people and has a strong, yet somewhat awkward, sense of justice. Coming from an upper-class family, she excels in school and always uses "teinei-go," a polite form of Japanese.

She likes younger guys and is quite fond of Negi, but hates impertinent, unruly boys like

Kotaro. Her brother died before birth, so it is speculated that Ayaka may somehow see something of him in Negi.

Ayaka has been a student at the Mahora Academy since her elementary school days when she met Asuna. They have fought like cats and dogs ever since. Though they may have this kind of relationship on the surface, they actually see each other as friends. When not staying at her lavish home, Ayaka rooms with Natsumi, Chizuru, and now Kotaro.

Nodoka Miyazaki

Nodoka is a silent, reserved, yet courageous girl who hides her face behind a thick veil of hair. Her love for books has earned her the nickname Honya, or "Bookstore," and she lives by the motto that if somebody likes reading, they must be a nice person. Being a non-athletic type, Nodoka also is prone to tripping and fainting when she is startled or overly embarrassed.

Honya makes up part of the Library Exploration Club along with Yue and Haruna, and gets along well with Konoka too. She has a great respect for Negi and came to have a crush on him. So far she has confessed her feelings for him twice, once during the class trip to Kyoto, and again at the school festival. Negi was flattered but seems confused about his own emotions so he hasn't given her a clean reply yet. This uncertainty hasn't but a strain in their relationship though and they continue to be good friends. On the fieldtrip, Nodoka and Negi formed a pactio when she won Chamo and Kazumi's contest to see who could be the first to kiss Negi. Nodoka later discovered the existence of magic and came to learn about Negi's bitter past.

Haruna Saotome

One of the extracurricular activities that Haruna takes part in is the Manga Club. Each month she rushes to complete her latest work on time and bothering her near the end of the deadline is ill-advised. She also takes part in the Library Exploration Club with Yue and Nodoka. She is very much attuned to and receptive of other people's emotions and often tries to help Nodoka win Negi's heart by forcing them into situations where they can be alone. Being the dramatic type, Haruna also loves gossip and is known for her ability to spread rumors from one end of campus to the other in a matter of hours, though her information is often flawed.

During the event at the Mahora Arena, Haruka learned about magic and Negi's being a mage. She also was able to find out more about Negi on the Internet and discovered his quest to find his missing father but she is unaware of his hometown's plight.

She made a contract with Negi on the second day of the school festival.

Yue Ayase

Yue's love for books but contempt for study lands her in the position of "Baka Black" the leader of the so-called "Baka Rangers". Despite this, she is a sharp young girl with profound insight into how the world works and can make accurate conjectures with little information. She is typically portrayed in a cool, calm manner though just a little too serious at times and never wants to bend the rules too far. Yue is a member of the Library Exploration Club along with Haruna and Nodoka.

Yue learned about magic and Negi's being a mage during the Kyoto fieldtrip, and works to support his cause by studying magic herself. With the urging of Haruna and Nodoka, Yue joined ranks as one of Negi's partners during the school festival story arc.

Kaede Nagase

Kaede is a six-foot tall ninja, training in the way of the Koga. She knows a variety of styles of ninjutsu and can readily control her own "ki", similar to Kansai region mages. Having trained in the mountains every weekend, Kaede's skill and technique has progressed to the level that it has even earned her praise from the mighty Albireo Imma doppelganger, Ku:Nel Sanders.

She generally takes life one day at a time, and it was this laidback attitude that contributed to her inclusion in the "Baka Rangers" as "Baka Blue." Kaeda lives with the Narutaki sisters and all of them are members of the school's Walking Club. She was the second to learn of Negi's magic when she saw him fly away on his staff after their mountain training. More recently, Kaede has also begun training with Kotaro.

Ku Fei

Ku Fei, a Chinese girl, is head of the Martial Arts Club and a master in Kenpo. Ever since her victory in the 2002 Martial Arts Tournament, she has become popular with the boys, albeit for fighting, and is challenged to fights on a daily basis.

Much like Kaede, her focus on fighting has caused her school grades to suffer, making her "Baka Yellow" of the "Baka Rangers." She does try her best when it comes to learning Japanese though.

Ku Fei is good friends with Chachamaru, Satomi and Satsuki, and Chao. During the school festival they all worked together to run the famous Chao Bao Zi Chinese restaurant.

Ku Fei, together with Mana, Kaede, and Setsuna, helped Negi during the Kyoto incident and it was at this time she learned of his magical background. Having returned to Tokyo, Negi began training with Ku Fei every morning to improve his combat capabilities.

Makie Sasaki

The sporty Makie is bright, cheerful, and has a passion for rhythmic gymnastics. She has been practicing since the age of five and is particularly talented with the ribbon. Makie's cooking is pretty good too but her study skills are terrible, making her "Baka Pink" in the "Baka Rangers."

Makie is good friends with the other athletes Yuna, Akira and Ako, whom she currently dorms with. She used to have affections for one of the members of her rhythmic gymnastics club, but she has recently taken a liking for her teacher, Negi. She used to only like Negi for his good looks but came to respect him for having clear-cut goals that he works hard to achieve.

On the second day of the school festival, Makie and some other students researched Negi on the Internet and discovered why he came to Japan in the first place.

Yuna Akashi

Yuna is a lively girl who always seems to be around when things start to go wrong. She is in the basketball club and is friends with fellow athletes Ako, Akira, and Makie. She has a liking for older men, and her father, Professor Akashi, is one of the campus's magic-using staff.

Her mother died when she was young, making Yuna feel responsible for her disheveled father. She tends to cook for him when at home and calls him every morning to check up on things.

Yuna placed fourth in the "Mars Vs. Mages" tournament on the third day of the school festival.

Ako Izumi

Ako is timid and gentle, but excels at sports. She told one of her upperclassmen that she liked him, but her feelings weren't returned. Adding to this painful memory, she also has a sizable scar on her back that she is very self-conscious about. In her class of superhuman students, Ako feels as though her normalness is her weakest point and it's this that keeps the aspiring rock star out of the forefront.

Ako thinks that Negi is cool for his focus and dedication and she is on good terms with her athletic classmates, Akira, Yuna, Makie, Madoka, and her roommate Makie. Ako has a thing for older men and was immediately taken in by Negi after he took age-deceiving pills. She made an attempt to tell him how she felt on the second day of the school festival, but ultimately succumbed to embarrassment.

Chisame Hasegawa

Chisame is a realist who doesn't get involved in fights she knows she can't win. It is this realistic way of thinking that keeps her from picking up on any of the eccentricities and supernatural abilities of her classmates. She is also known to be uncooperative, unfriendly, and to have a careless and often rude way of speaking, sometimes forgetting to use polite speech in front of teachers. All in all, Chisame is a rather distant person, but in the end she'll help out if she needs to.

She appears to be a normal, rule-abiding girl on the outside, but behind closed doors she becomes Net Idol Chu and keeps a webpage with pictures of her in different costumes and suggestive poses. As a self-proclaimed Super Hacker, Chisame has the ability to artificially alter the flow of internet traffic, leaving her site ranked as the best. She is so absorbed by cosplay that if she sees another person with a poorly made costume, she'll remake it just to satisfy herself.

Chisame learned of magic at

the Mahora Arena and made a contract with Negi on the third day of the school festival.

Fuka Narutaki

Fuka is Fumika's older twin sister. Both she and her sister are short and most people don't even realize they are Secondary School students. She uses this to her advantage to get child-rates at movie theaters, but also seems to hate this stereotype and has gotten a hold of a machine that is supposed to help her grow taller. Unlike Fumika, Fuka is a little tomboyish and has a wilder side to her personality.

Fuka's roommates are Fumika and Kaede, and all three of them belong to the Walking Club. Fuka, Fumika, and Shiina never seem to get left out and are always part of the action.

Fumika Narutaki

Fumika is Fuka's younger twin sister, but she is comparatively more mature. Fumika's room-mates are Fuka and Kaede, and all three of them belong to the Walking Club. She respects Kaede a lot and may even be learning ninjutsu from her. Fumika, Fuka, and Shiina never seem to get left out and are always part of the action.

Evangeline A. K. McDowell

At first glance she may look like a cute, innocent, 10-year-old girl, but she is actually a power-ful species of vampire known as Shinso (high daylight walker), who has roamed the earth for hundreds of years.

Evangeline was born in Europe and restricted to life in a castle until her 10th birthday when she became a vampire. In order to extract revenge on the man who did this to her, she left her castle for a country where she could learn the art of magic. She doesn't associate herself with any one country, and had most recently resided on a solitary island in the South Seas where she stayed in isolation. Currently, she lives together with Chachamaru in her own house on the Mahora Academy campus. Evangeline doesn't get along particularly well with other students and is usually only accompanied by her robotic assistant. As she has been trapped on campus for the past 15 years, she has grown tired of repeating the same class and often plays hooky.

The magic Nagi used to bind Evangeline and seal her powers is of exceptional strength. Because of this, her life isn't much different from that of an ordinary 10 year old, but on the full moon some of her magic abilities return, along with her fangs.

In her 100 years since arriving in Japan, Evangeline has had ample time to learn and perfect Aikitessen, giving her well-rounded magic abilities of the utmost quality. She has come to appreciate her vampire-heritage to a certain degree and to think of humans as inferior creatures.

The A. K. in Evangeline A. K. McDowell stands for Athanasia Katherine.

Chachamaru Karakuri

Chachamaru is Evangeline's battle-ready robotic assistant who is powered by a combination of magic and Satomi's AI programming. She is Evangeline's Magistra Magi and always refers to her owner as "Master." Chachamaru was designed and built by Satomi along with Chacha Zero and various other robots.

For Chachamaru, Evangeline's orders are absolute and she typically acts in accordance, however she is known to tease Evangeline on occasion too. Satomi's orders are also absolute, but it is unknown whose orders have priority.

With boosters installed on her back and in her legs, Chachamaru is able to fly for short periods of time and is often seen equipped with heavy weaponry. Recently, she has become self-conscious and has developed somewhat of a fashion sense, making it seem as though she has found a way to alter her original programming.

Chachamaru was one of the first to know of Negi's being a mage, and she also worked at the Chao Bao Zi Chinese restaurant during the school festival.

Madoka Kugimiya

Madoka is a member of the Reading Club. She rooms with Misa and Sakurako and is often with her and fellow cheerleader and friend Ako. Madoka has a short fuse and when her club mates get out of control she often has to settle them down. Her nicknames include Kugimi and Kugimin but she doesn't seem to care for either of them.

Sakurako Shiina

Sakurako is a bubbly girl with a cute smile and a passion for gambling. She is in the Cheerleading Club and dorms with Misa and Madoka and is often seen with the Narutaki twins. Sakurako dreamed of one day owning a cake shop when she was younger.

Misora Kasuga

As a Christian, Misora actively practices as a nun at the on-campus church. Despite this, she also has a mischievous side and likes to pull pranks. Misora is able to use magic and her parents encourage her to do so, but she isn't motivated and hasn't been able to develop her skill.

Misora and her friend Cocone both work under the direction of Sister Shakti but the details of their duties are fuzzy. As the Ministra Magi to Cocone, Misora's artifact is a pair of sneakers that allow her to run at superhuman speeds.

Setsuna Sakurazaki

Setsuna is a half-demon, her demon half being a bird. While her status in the bird clan was quite high, she was born with white wings, which are taboo in that culture. Because of this, she was forced to leave her village and headed for Kyoto, where she met Eishun, Konoka's father. There she trained in the way of the Kyoto Shinmei-ryu style of sword fighting and quickly hit it off with Konoka.

Over time, training Setsuna became more and more focused on training, and slowly she and Konoka began to drift apart. By the time she was a teenager, Setsuna's proficiency in Shinmei-ryu was obvious, so Eishun decided to put her in charge of Konoka's protection when she entered the Mahora Academy. At that time, Konoka didn't know that Setsuna was a half-demon, and she feared that if she ever found out, she would come to detest her. Because of this, she preferred to distance herself from Konoka and watch her from the shadows instead. During the class trip to Kyoto, however, Setsuna was forced to make the split-second decision to change into her winged form in order to save Konoka's life. Embarrassed and shamed, she tried to run away but Negi and Asuna were able to talk her out of it at the last minute. Setsuna and Konoka have been good friends ever since, but she still insists on addressing Konoka as "Ojo-sama", a title used for young ladies of high social status.

Setsuna's fighting abilities are amplified by her half-demon heritage, and this has earned her praise from even Evangeline. She is also able to control "ki" and the Onmyou style of magic. Her sword's name is Yunagi, which translates into "Evening Calm."

She was the third person to make a probationary contract

with Negi. She wishes to make one with Konoka as well, but didn't feel comfortable making the ritual kiss, though Konoka said herself that she wouldn't mind.

Kazumi Asakura

Kazumi is a young reporter for the Mahora Newspaper who is always on the lookout for the next juicy story. She has been called the "Mahora Paparazzi" by some, and thrives on collecting as much information as she can about her fellow classmates. As a journalist, Kazumi is respected by those around her with her strong sense of justice and belief in the power of action. She is able to collect information stealthily and easily, and also excels as a public speaker, acting as an announcer during school events or as a chairman in meetings.

Kazumi found out about Negi's being a mage during the fieldtrip to Kyoto and wanted to go public with it, but gave up on the idea with the urging of Chamo. Today, she works for Negi as a secret agent of sorts and hopes to one day make a probationary contract with him so she can have an artifact too.

After two years of sitting next to Sayo's haunted seat, Kazumi is now able to see and interact with her paranormal classmate. They have become friends and Sayo helps Kazumi collect information by using her ghostly-ness to her advantage to sneak into the middle of private conversations.

Mana Tatsumiya

Despite being a secondary school student, Mana is well established as an expert marksman and mercenary who always carries out her jobs with coldhearted ambition. She has difficulties talking about her own past, but that might have something to do with the death of her Magister Magi back in 2001. During that time she was able to travel extensively though her work at an NGO (non-governmental organization) that rescues helpless people from war-ravaged regions.

Aside from her freelance mercenary work, Mana also holds a part-time job as a shrine maiden at the on-campus Tatsumiya Shrine. She knows about the existence of magic and Negi's being a mage. She rooms with Setsuna.

Natsumi Murakami

Natsumi has serious insecurities with her freckled face and red hair. She sees herself as just an ordinary girl who doesn't really stand out among all of the cute girls in her class. Rooming with the beautiful Ayaka and mature-looking Chizuru doesn't do anything to help her confidence either. Recently, she has taken an interest in Kotaro after he began living with them.

Chizuru Naba

Chizuru likes to move at her own pace and is depicted as being slightly absent minded. However, she does have a strong opinion on things and takes a stand against nonsensical rules and ideas.

She hopes to be a day-care worker in the future and volunteers at an on-campus facility as a companion and role model for misbehaving children. Chizuru looks older than she actually is, but gets angry if told so.

She found Kotaro when he was wounded and unconscious on the street and allowed him to stay with her while he was recovering. He later transferred to the Mahora Academy and continues to live with her, Ayaka, and Natsumi.

Satsuki Yotsuba

Satsuki is a natural cook who dreams of one day opening up her own shop and it is because of this clear, obtainable goal that makes her the only student in the class that is respected by Evangeline. She is popular with university students and staff alike because of her innocent and friendly disposition, earning her the nickname "Sa-chan."

During the school festival, Satsuki helps to run the famous Chao Bao Zi restaurant with Chachamaru, Chao, Satomi, and Ku Fei. It is possible that she may know of the existence of magic having worked so closely with Satomi and Chao.

Sayo Aisaka

Sayo died in 1940 at the young age of 15 and her spirit continues to roam the halls of the Mahora Secondary School to this day. The seat she used to occupy in the front of the classroom is said to be haunted and anyone who sits in it claims to feel a sudden, noticeable chill. The circumstances surrounding Sayo's death are a mystery and nobody knows what unfinished business her restless spirit may still have in this world.

Her presence is rather weak making it hard for even psychic mediums to see her. Typically, only other supernatural beings such as Evangeline seem to be able to sense her presence, with the exception of Kazumi, who can from having sat next to her vacant seat for the past two years. However, others can also see Sayo on days when she is feeling particularly well, though her image tends to be horrifyingly crude and ghost-like.

While Sayo might sound spooky, she is actually quite harmless. For a ghost, she is quite timid and all she wants to do it make some friends. She was eventually able to develop a relationship with Kazumi and often helps her collect information for her articles.

Zazie Rainyday

Zazie is a foreign exchange student whose dark skin is

accented by her white hair. She is a member of the Magic and her usually silent and expressionless face lights up during performances. Among other abilities, she is skilled at the trapeze and also has a way with birds. Zazie has many mysterious friends and is somehow able to see Sayo without any problems.

Satomi Hakase

Satomi is a science-loving girl who has no other interests outside of her own research. Because of this, those who know her have dubbed her "Hakase," which is a play on her last name and means "doctor" or "professor." She has a habit of doing questionable things in the name of science and this has lead to rumor that she may be a mad scientist similar to Chao.

Satomi and Chao both belong to the university's engineering department and rent a laboratory together, which more often than not doubles as a bedroom. By only focusing on her work, Satomi has a complete disregard for neatness and often leaves her lab in disarray with clothing scattered in various locations.

Every year Satomi helps Chachamaru, Satsuki, Ku Fei, and Chao with the operation of the famous Chao Boa Zi Chinese restaurant. As Chachamaru's creator, she is also charged with her maintenance. She knew of magic and Negi's being a mage from the very beginning.

Chao Lingshen

Chao is a perfectionist when it comes to anything from study, to sports, to cooking. She has the highest GPA in the class and many even think she may be one of the smartest on campus. Like Satomi she has come up with a variety of useful inventions, but she is also thought to be somewhat of a mad scientist with her obsession for science. Chao also belongs to the Chinese Martial

Arts Club and is pals with Ku Fei.

Aside from that, she is the owner of the popular Chao Bao Zi Chinese restaurant and works hard with Ku Fei, Satomi, Satsuki, and Chachamaru when it opens for the school festival. Negi liked the Chinese meatbuns at her restaurant so much that he contributed to their being introduced in the UK.

Chao is a mysterious girl who has had various run-ins with the teacher at her school ever since entering two years before Negima! takes place. She talks Negi's decedents into coming from the future to change the past, but the details of this claim are unknown.

Misa Kakizaki

Misa is good friends with fellow cheerleaders Sakurako and Madoka. She is the only one in the class to have a steady boyfriend but after seeing how Negi will look in the future she sets her "Reverse Hikaru Genji" plan into motion to get him interested in older girls. Hikaru Genji is the protagonist in the classic Japanese story The Tale of Genji He was an aristocrat who had a particularly liking toward young girls.

Akira Okouchi

Akira excels at sports and is the most valued member of the school's Swimming Club. All of that training must have paid off because she is strong enough to lift with Negi and Yuna with only one arm. She is a good friend with fellow athletes Yuna, Makie, and Ako and secretly fawns over Negi.

Characters Tied to Negi:

Albert Chamomile

This lecherous ermine fled to Japan to avoid being arrested

for stealing over 2,000 pairs of girls' underwear and now lodges in Asuna's room. While Negi's magic academy punishes troublemaking mages by turning them into ermines, Chamo is the real thing deal - except that he is magical and can speak. He formed a strong relationship with Negi after being rescued from a trap by the boy and affectionately refers to him as "Aniki," or "older brother."

Nekane Springfield

Nekane and Negi have a complex relationship. Nekane is actually a cousin of Negi's despite the fact that he refers to her as his sister. In addition to this, the much older Nekane took care of him when he was younger so is something of a mother figure for him as well.

Her village was attacked by demons six years before the story of Negima! takes place, and her legs were turned to stone in the ensuing battle as she tried to protect Negi. As an aftereffect, it is thought that she may now rely on prosthetic legs for mobility.

Nekane currently works as a faculty member of a magic academy and keeps in touch with Negi by sending him letters every now and then. She is able to use magic, but the extent of her abilities is unknown.

Anna Yurieuna Cocorowa

Also known by the name Anya, she is one year older than Negi but graduated from the Merdiana Magic Academy at the same time. She graduated early having skipped one grade whereas Negi graduated having skipped two. After graduation she was sent to London to train as a fortuneteller.

Anya comes across as a precocious girl and often speaks ill of Negi, but also admires his dedicated spirit and enjoys his company. She is jealous of Asuna's relationship with Negi.

Anya's specialization in the realm of fire based magic.

Merdiana Magic Academy Headmaster

The headmaster is an older gentleman with long hair and a moustache. Negi refers to him as "grandpa" but it's not known if they are related by blood. Likewise, his name is yet to be revealed. The Merdiana Magic Academy Headmaster is a friend Mahora Academy's dean, Kono-emon and Donet McGuiness is thought to have a pactio with him.

Stan

Stan is an older mage from the town in Wales that Negi used to live in. He is of a strong but silent disposition and considers himself a friend of Negi's father, though he didn't particularly care for Nagi's reckless antics when they were younger. When Nagi disappeared, Stan vowed

to look after his son.

Stan has the power to seal evil spirits within magic bottles and was the one to initially imprison Herrman, but was turned to stone in the process and remains so even today.

Kotaro Inugami

Kataro is the young wolf half-demon who is able to summon the tormented Inugami spirits to fight by his side. He is able to change into a form reminiscent of a werewolf in which case his natural fighting abilities are amplified. He retains his pointed ears and tail even when not in his werewolf form. Moreover, he can also revert to a dog form as when the girls of Mahora Academy found him on the verge of death.

As a half-demon, life has been rough for the young Kotaro. He has spent most of his life alone. Originally, he teamed up with Chigusa to defeat Negi, but was defeated by Kaede during the Kyoto story arc. Kotaro was placed under house arrest for his embarrassing defeat, but later escaped to the Mahora Academy to warn Negi of Herrman's release. In the end, he was injured and couldn't make it to Negi in time, but later assisted with resealing the demon in his magical prison.

Kotaro was able to enroll in the Mahora Academy, but it's not known what his current grade level is. He is rooming with Chizuru, Ayaka, and Natsumi under the guise of her younger brother to avoid suspicion. He never fights with Ayaka and is suspected of having a crush on her.

He never had contact with people his age up until the point when he arrived at the Mahora Academy and has taken up a something of a friendly rivalry with Negi and always pushes him to try harder. Kotaro is self-taught in the art of fighting but now takes lessons along-side Negi at Evangeline's villa to polish his skills.

Chacha Zero

Chacha Zero is a long-time assistant of Evengelines's whose form resembles that of a marionette. Unlike her other assistant Chachamaru, Chacha Zero is animated entirely by Evangeline's magic and because of this, she is restricted to the confines of the imprisoning magical boundary around the academy.

While Evengeline has settled down since entering the academy, Chacha Zero character is a remnant of her former cruel, sadistic self. She equips herself with large knives and can move freely in areas with large concentrations of magic, such as the Evangeline's Resort and during the school festival when the World Tree was accumulating power.

The Crimson Wing Forces

Nagi Springfield

Negi's father is widely known as the hero of the great magic war. His power is legendary and it is said that he earned his alias the "Thousand Master" because of his supposed proficiency of one thousand spells. As a battle mage, Nagi also demonstrated mastery in martial arts, making him powerful to the point that the assistance of Magistra Magi simply wasn't necessary.

In terms of sheer magical might, his superiority is unquestionable, however, Evangeline's own accounts of the man seem to contradict some of the rumors surrounding him. According to her, Nagi claimed to know only five or six spells, which was the reason for his studying hand-to-hand combat: if he wanted to use other spells during battle he would need a way to hold off enemies while he looked up the correct incantations.

Nagi imprisoned the evil-doing Evangeline at the Mahora Academy with a powerful barrier that sapped her magical power in what he called "Attendance Hell." He had promised to free her from her prison after she graduated from school, but five years later he was rumored to have died.

According to official records, Nagi died in 1993 but Negi claims that he saved him in 1997 when Herrman attacked their village. If currently alive, Nagi would be 35 years old when the story takes place because he had appeared 25 years ago in the last Mahora Martial Arts Tournament at the age of 10.

Nagi's mischievous personality stands in contrast to his well-mannered and hard working son. Evidently, Nagi has reappeared to Albireo to prove his still lives, but has yet to do so with Negi or Evangeline.

Eishun Konoe

Eishun was once a member of Nagi's Crimson Wing squad. He is an accomplished Shinmei-ryu swordsman and helped fight in the great magic war of years past. When the dust had settled, he separated ways with Nagi and began work as the leader of the Kansai Magic Association but he still bares injuries from his earlier days. He actually married into the Konoe family and it isn't his real last name.

Eishun had wanted his daughter Konoka to grow up to lead a normal life free of the influence of magic, but Chigusa dashed this hope when she abducted her. He later forgave Chigusa and her group of rebel, having become soft with years of conflict free life.

Eishun also falls into the category of rugged men that Asuna likes so much. The sword he used during the great magical war, Yunagi, has been handed down to Setsuna. He won't tell Asuna the truth behind Takamichi's past until she is older.

Gateau Vanderburg

Gateau was one of the original members of the Crimson Wing. Takamichi looks similar to how he did, smokes a lot like he did, and was also a student of Gateau. He was a master of the Kanka, or "Magic Ki Fusion" style of combat. Gateau is currently thought to have passed away.

Asuna traveled with the Crimson Wing group when she was a child and at that time she didn't seem to care for Gateau, but she cried when she was told that he had sustained a fatal wound and was separated from their party. Gateau was more than likely the driving influence that later caused Asuna to develop a liking for rough men and the smell of cigarette smoke.

Albireo Imma

Albireo was one of the original members of the Crimson Wing.

He is a handsome man with flowing hair whose appearance has hardly changed in the past 20 years. He entered the Mahora Fighter's Tournament under the alias of "Ku:Nel Sanders" and likely enjoys the taste of fried chicken. He has astounding powers and has had to use them on both Kotaro and Kaede. In combat, he chiefly uses gravity magic, but is also skilled in hand-to-hand combat. Aside from this, he also demonstrated his deep knowledge of healing magic when he was able to fix Ku Fei's broken arm with the tip of his finger.

Although he used to go by Al, he only responds to Ku:Nel at the tournament. The reason for this is because this isn't Albireo's true form, but a double that can only emerge during the annual school festival. His actual self has been hidden away, slumbering, for the past 10 years somewhere on campus. During the tournament, Evangeline recognized Ku:Nel to be Albireo at once and said that they are old acquaintances and she expects that, like her, he may not be mortal.

Albireo holds a contract with the Thousand Master and his pactio card is called Bibliothecariaironicus. The card is still active, which is proof that Nagi still lives. He also holds a number of other dead pactio cards with deceased mages.

Big Sword Man

This guy belonged to the Crimson Wing. He had a really big sword.

Other Students in the Mahora Academy

Takane D. Goodman

Takane is one of the magic-using members of the Saint Ursula All-Girls High School.

During the school festival, she was one of the members who were called to the World Tree by Konoemon to prevent the misuse of its magical power. She has a straightforward, discipline-oriented, way of thinking and often gets on Negi's case when he misbehaves and she entered the tournament in order to show him who is boss.

Specializing in shadow magic, Takane is able to summon up to 17 shadow warriors that she can manipulate in combat and can also use the secret technique "Black Clothing Nocturne." Additionally, she can use shadows to bolster her physical capabilities, making her stronger than normal humans, and was capable of rocketing her robot opponent into the air during the tournament.

Takane graduated from magic school and came to Mahora Academy after having lived in America. She has a pure heart and soon plans to use her magic to help the people of the world. It's her goal to become powerful Magister Magi like the Thousand Master.

Mei Sakura

Mei is one of the magic using students of the Mahora Secondary School. She is a straight-A student who is currently studying magic at a school in America and has recently learned how to cast chant-less spells. She is also attuned to her surroundings and was the first to notice the flying robots Chao was using to spy on the teacher meeting near the World Tree. Her specialization is in fire-based magic but her fighting skills are still a work in progress.

Mei has a close relationship with Takane, who is her Magister Magi, and her artifact is a broom.

Megumi Natsume

Megumi's nickname is "Natsumegu" and she is a member of

the Mahora Secondary School Drama Club. She can also use magic. She wears glasses and has long braids that frame her face on both sides. She is often seen with a staff and specializes in water-based magic.

Cocone

Cocone is an elementary school student with a keen sense of hearing and is a capable magic-user. She is Misora's Minister Magi and they are often seen together. Cocone resembles Mana with her dark skin and red eyes but it's not known if they are related. She has a laid back personality and speaks in monotone. Like Misora, Cocone is also a student of Sister Shakti.

Eiko

Eiko is a student of the Mahora Saint Ursula High School and captain of the dodge ball team the Black Lilies. She is friends with Bibi and Shii and is liked by Naoya, a boy from a different school's dodge ball team.

Serizawa

He is the captain of the university biathlon team that Mana belongs to. He was going to confess his love for her at the school festival, but she shot him in the head instead. He bears a resemblance to her deceased Magister Magi.

Pochi Digouin

He fought in the Fighters Tournament, but lost to Ku:Nel Sander in the first round. His fighting style is Kenpo and he is able to project his attacks. He hasn't seen much action in the series

Kaoru Goutokuji

He is a young man who participated in the martial arts tournament. He uses an original style of fighting and is able to control the flow of ki in his body. He is rather capable for a normal person and was even able to offset some of Negi's magical attacks. He is a hot-blooded yet shy young man and a good sport as he later went on to cheer for Negi.

Tsuji

The head of the kendo club. He was in the D group and was one of the last three people remaining. He was defeated by Ku Fei after smacking him on the head. Judging from the few words he uttered, it sounds like this may not have been their first fight.

Tatsuya Nakamura

A fighter in the martial arts tournament who is able to use powerful projectile attacks. He fought against Kaede and while he lost because of his lack of close combat skills, his skill did earn him some praise.

Keichi Yamashita

A fighter in the Martial Arts Tournament who specializes in "3D Jiujutsu." He fought against Evangeline and knocked out as soon as the match started with one swift blow.

Haruki

A young boy in the Mahora Elementary School. He may not have a way with words but he does have a thing for a girl in his school named Yuki. During the school festival he wore a polar bear suit and sold "polar bear crepes." Yuki confessed having feelings for him but they are still young and not sure if they are actually a couple or not.

Yuki

A young girl in the Mahora Elementary School. She confessed having feelings for Yuki but they aren't sure if they are actually dating yet. During the school festival they won the best couple contest.

Nanaka Airheart

A member of the university

Aviation Club. She piloted a plane for the school festival's opening event and made an announcement from a biplane. According to Chizuru, she also confirmed that Chao was on top of the blimp during the closing event.

Things created by magic

Golem

He was the protector of the Book of Melchizedek in Library Island. When the Baka Rangers came to steal the book to study for their exam, he forced them to play English Twister. In the end, it is learned that the Konoemon was behind the whole deal.

Chibi Setsuna

A shikigami used by Setsuna that resembles her and wears the clothing of the Karasu Tengu. She is equipped with a miniature version of the Yunagi, but it's blade is on par with that of a fruit knife. She shares consciousness with and can be controlled by Setsuna over long distances. She communicates with Setsuna primarily by telepathy.

The Sword Goddess

A golem created by Haruna Saotome using her pactio artifact. The Goddess's upper body is that of a woman with armor and her arms are two massive swords. Her lower body is skirt-shaped and her legs are indistinguishable. She has the fighting skills one would expect of one of Haruna's masterpieces. She had originally drawn only one arm to fight against the giant dog, but later added the other one to fight Chachamaru's clone.

There is one other golem that Haruka uses that has the ability to use fire spells. It has long tentacles and bears the image of a sinister looking Nodoka.

Seven Electronic Spirits

They are the seven digitized spirits who reside in the online world and are controlled by Chisame's artifact Sceptrum Virtuale. Each spirit has 1,000 minions and the highest ranking of the seven is able to communicate directly with the artifacts user. Each of the seven spirits are supposed to be given a name by their master but Chisame didn't feel like doing it so she left it up to Makie. They are able to appear in the real world and are evidentially capable of eating.

Negi's Enemies

Chigusa Amagasaki

She is an Inyou user from the Kansai Onmyou Association who wears glasses and makes use of a giant doll-like monkey and bear demon to protect her. She also employs the use of frog and swallow shikigami. Both of her parents were lost in the great magic war and ever since then she has felt resentment toward Western Mages. She often uses paper seals in battle and is familiar with a variety of magic including fire and water-based.

Kishin, Usoku, and Kitsuneme

They are summoned monsters that Chigusa called with Konoka's power in an attempt to get Negi off of her tail. There were roughly 150 demons that appeared with the majority of them being Kishin, followed by Usoku and Kitsuneme. Asuna was able to deal with the Kishin, but the Usoku proved to be a more difficult challenge in the end.

Tsukuyomi

She studies in the same Shinmei-ryu style of sword fighting that Setsuna does but fights with a sword in each hand, which makes her better suited for close combat. She is capable of summoning a large number of shikigami and loves fighting; especially if her opponent is a woman. Her glasses sometimes slip down her face in battle, which can lead to her making a mistake.

Fate Averruncus

He is the young white-haired boy who was helping Chigusa in attempting to kidnap Konoka during the Kyoto story arc. He appears to be Negi's age but his true identity and form are unknown. According to Evangeline, he is closer to a puppet than a human and was likely created by and serves somebody with great magical power. Among others, he specializes in water-based magic, is well versed in martial arts, and was powerful enough to infiltrate the barrier around the Kansai Onmyou Association without any problems. At present, his strength is far greater than Negi's.

He came to Japan after training with the Istanbul Magic Association and was in Japan one month before the start of the Kyoto fieldtrip for training.

Ryome Suku no Kami

A legendary demon from Japan's past. He is an enormous 60 meters tall and has two faces and four arms and legs. He was summoned by Chigusa during the Kyoto story arc using Konoka's latent magical power. Despite all of the hype surrounding him, he was easily defeated by Evangeline after which he was once again sealed by Eishun.

Ryome Suku no Kami had escaped one other time 18 years ago but at that time was sealed inside a giant stone by Eishun and Nagi.

Dragon of Library Island

A scary fire-breathing dragon residing deep inside Library Island. It has no arms but instead has claws at the end of its wings like that of a bat and according to Yue it is technically a wyvern. Negi has fought it on two occasions. On the first encounter Negi wasn't powerful enough to defeat it and simply ran away. Even with the necessary skills it would still take days to topple the beast.

Wilhelm Josef Von Herrman

He is a high-ranking demon who was once a powerful aristocrat but is now working for somebody else. He is highly skilled in magic and specializes in petrifaction based spells. He says that the only thing he likes more than talented people is destroying them but he isn't completely even and, for now, is content to just test Negi's skill.

He was one of many demons who attacked Negi's home village six years before the story takes place and was the one responsible for turning over half of the townsfolk to stone. Stan was able to seal him in a magical bottle but Herrman was able to escape sometime later with a little help. During the fight with Negi he made use of Asuna's magic-canceling powers to negate Negi's attack.

Ameko, Suramui, and Purin

Also known as the Three Slime Sisters, these three are can move on their own volition and are able to change their shape allowing them to imitate others. Ameko wears glasses and uses polite speech. Suramui and Purin are both rude but Saramui is cheerful whereas Purin shows little expression.

They are fast on their feet and capable of striking quickly and are said to eat people on occasion by dissolving their flesh. They can also teleport using water as a median and are fond of the spell "Water Dungeon," which they use to incapacitate people.

They are currently trapped once again inside the magic

bottle after having been sealed there by Nodoka and Yue.

T-ANK-α3 aka Tanaka

Tanaka is a military robot created by the Mahora Robotics Club. Its two main ways of fighting are using a beam that is fired from its mouth and a rocket punch, though Satomi has said that the beam isn't powerful enough to take somebody's life. On the last day of the school festival Chao released an army of 2,500 mass-produced Tanaka robots to wreck havoc on the Mahora Academy campus. The one used in the Martial Arts Tournament was connected to a power supply, but the ones that appeared later were all animated with magic from the World Tree.

Other Characters

Taizo Ayase

Yue's late grandfather, who was a famous philosopher. She respected him greatly and he had a big influence on her life. He passed away around the same time Yue entered the Mahora Secondary School.

Ayaka's Servants

The people who work at the Yukihiro household. They include an old butler, a chauffeur, and a large number of maids.

The Konoe Estate Shrine Maidens

The people working at the Konoe Family home, which is also the Kansai Onmyou Association's headquarters. While they wear the garments of priestesses, they appear to act more like maids as they were the ones to help entertain Negi and his students when they visited the Konoe home. They were all turned to stone when Fate infiltrated the headquarters but Konoka was able to heal them in the end.

Donet McGuiness

She is a magic user who first appeared with the Merdiana headmaster when Negi was explaining the idea of Minister Magi to Asuna. Some people think that she may be the head-master's Minister Magi. Donet is a friend of Yuna's mother and she helped her father to gather information on Fate.

Donet is English, had beautiful blonde hair and is fluent in Japanese. At first glance she looks as though she may be a stern person but is actually quite friendly. Yuna had mistaken her for dating her father.

Zazie's friends

They assisted Zazie in class 3-A's haunted house during the school festival. At this time Zazie was overheard telling them not to "eat the customers," so there is a good chance that they may not be human. They wear black clothes and strange masks and were able to become friends with Chisame at Chao's farewell party.

Magic

When we hear the word "magic," we tend to think about the witches and wizards depicted in picture books and fairy tales. An example of this is the Brothers Grimm's Fairy Tales. This is a collection of stories handed down through the generations since its first publication in the 19th century and has influenced many stories that followed. These days, titles such as The Lord of the Rings, Earthsea and, more recently, Harry Potter have taken the original tales into contemporary mainstream settings.

If you look up the word "magic" in a dictionary, you will find a description of it as some sort of mysterious power. Similarly, the word "magician" is used for somebody who is able to perform the seemingly impossible. "Magic" has its origins in Greek where it was spelled as "magike" and then later as "magik" when it was adopted into the English language.

There are many other words such as "sorcery", "wizardry", and "witchcraft" that can also be used to describe mysterious powers. Likewise, in Japan and other eastern countries there are also a wide variety of words that can be used to explain different styles of magic.

In the past, if an unexplainable phenomenon took place, people reasoned that it must be the work of a higher power, and before long, religions were formed that offered explanations. With this came the concept of gods and thus people who desired godly powers, and this may be how the idea of magic was first formed. Magic isn't something that cropped up in any one place but rather had a ubiquitous beginning and left an impact on many different cultures. In Negima! we see magic reflected not only in western and onmyou magic, but also in old martial arts such as kenpo and ninjutsu.

The idea of magic has had a huge impact on popular culture, but here it is recognized as fiction and is usually depicted in a "Western" sense. There are various types of Western magic, but using magic in Negima! requires the user to borrow the power of spirits; the spell Sagitta Magica (Magic Arrows) borrows spiritual power from light and lightning and the spell Flans Paries Venti Vertentis (Blow Forth, Wall of Churning Wind) borrows spiritual power from wind.

In Western magic each element is represented by a special spirit: Salamander is the spirit of fire; Undine is the spirit of water; Gnome is the spirit of earth; and Sylph is the spirit of wind. This is an ancient Greek idea that was introduced by Aristotle and remained popular well into Europe's Middle Ages and formed the building blocks for alchemy. Negima! makes good use of these four basic elements but also throws lightening and darkness into the mix.

This plays into the idea of animism; the idea that all things, whether animate or inanimate, possess a soul or spirit. Animism was a part of Celtic magic, but it was also firmly rooted in Chinese and Japanese beliefs and it helps to give an unexpected amount of depth to the story of Negima!.

Negi's attack magic

Fighting style

Western Mages fight with either their Minister Magi defending them from the front line so that they can cast support magic from the rear, or fight together with the Minister Magi while intermittently casting spells. The portrayal of this fighting mage is common in Negima! and seems to be the style of choice for many of the high level mages. Negi also wants to become a combat mage having been inspired by his father.

Magic Arrows

For this spell, spiritual energy is gathered and cast forth in a narrow beam of energy. Magic arrows can use a variety elemental energy including light, wind, lightning, darkness, water and fire. The spell can be cast either in multiples or the energy can be focused into one powerful blast. It's most commonly cast in multiple, primary numbers. This is the first spell learned in magic schools in Wales, and can be used as a chant-less spell.

When different elements are used with the spell, they have different effects. For example, light will cause destruction, lightning will cause electric shock or start fires. Likewise the wind element can be used to restrain people, water can be turned into ice, and darkness can be used to fire mysterious dark black bullets. Negi also developed a way to combine the magic arrow's power into his fist, which delivers a devastating punch.

Disarmament Spell

This spell delivers a great gust of wind that can disarm opponents without injuring them but can be used with other elements besides wind. The one Negi uses has the effect of blowing enemies' clothing off, turning it into flower petals. At the beginning of the story Negi accidentally released this spell when he sneezed, blowing the clothing off of anybody that happened to be around him. He has since improved his control of the spell. Evangeline also uses this spell but with an ice effect that freezes her opponents weapons and clothing.

Blow Forth, Dancing Dust

Powerful wind magic in the form of a cyclone. It's invoked by chanting, "Blow forth, dancing dust!"

Jupiter's Storm of Thunder

It's one of Negi's most powerful spells and sends a strong gust of wind and lightning barreling down on his enemy. The clant is rather long but Negi has managed to use it once against Evangeline, again in Kyoto, and for a third time to decide the battle against Chao. It was also shown being used by Nagi on one occasion to blow away part of a mountain. The chant for the spell is, "Come, spirits of air and lightning, O southern storm which blows with lightning! Jupiter's Storm of Thunder!"

Evoke; Summon

A spell used to summon elemental spirits. Negi has used it to summon Valkyrie wind spirits and the Lance and Sword Salamander spirits. More than one Sword Salamander can't be summoned at one time and it takes the appearance of the one who summoned it. It is useful for capturing people and for launching an ambush.

White Lightning

It is cast as a violent bolt of electricity that shoots from its user's hand. It's not very effective against inanimate objects but is very powerful if used against living things. The chant for the spell is, "A bolt of lightning to cut through the night, spring forth from my hand and strike my enemy! White Lightning!"

Magic Barrier

A protective barrier from physical and magical attacks. Negi specializes in wind-based magic so his barriers are made of wind. It's weaker than the wall of wind he can make, but it can be used for an extended period of time.

Magic Boost

Magic boost happens when magic is channeled from a magic user to his/her partner, adding to defense and bolstering natural abilities. The spell is invoked by uttering a partner's name and the amount of time the boost will be good for. This spell can be used on multiple people, on one's self, and can even be invoked on the Minister Magi's own volition. The results can vary when a mage uses magic boost on his or her self though.

Blow Forth, Wall of Wind

This spell is a wall that can protect against physical attacks and could even stop a ten-ton truck. The spell's shortcoming, however, is that it cannot be cast in quick succession but the spell is short and can be cast fast enough to block an imminent attack.

Blow Forth, Wall of Churning Wind

This spell summons a powerful tornado that can guard its caster for a matter of minutes. It was used by Negi in Kyoto to protect his group from a horde of enemies and while the outside of the tornado naturally had violent winds, the eye of the tornado was comparatively calm. Conversely it can also be used to trap enemies as used by Kataragi. The spell is invoked by uttering, "O turning storm of spring, bestow your aerial protection upon us! Blow Forth, Wall of Churning Wind!"

Axe of Lightning

A high level spell that is cast in an ancient language, which strikes an enemy from above with a powerful blast of lightening. According to Evangeline, Nagi liked to use the spell as a followup to a chant-less Magic Arrow attack to finish off his opponent. Aside from Nagi, Negi and Evangeline can use this spell. The spell is invoked by uttering, "Come forth from the void, O Thunder, and cut down my enemy! Axe of Lightning!"

Sleep-Inducing Fog

Magic fog that puts one's enemy to sleep. The spell is invoked by uttering, "Air and water, become a fog and grant a short rest to these people! Sleep-Inducing Fog!"

Wind Barrier

A spell that uses air to construct a mid-sized barrier around a certain area that can protect people from attacks by fire, poison gas, and sound. The spell works by condensing the air around it making it hard to the touch like a kind of potential barrier.

Restraining Magic

Negi used this spell when he fought Evangeline and Chachamaru and was able to immobilize them. He used the spell as a trap that was only triggered when they walked over it but they were able to cancel the spell with Chachamaru's magic canceling tool. The effect is a lot like the wind-based Magic Arrow.

Offensive Magic of Others

Evangeline A. K. McDowell

Ice Shield

A spell that can be used to block magical attacks. Evangeline uses this spell because she specializes in ice-based magic.

Magic Barrier

Unlike the Ice Shield spell, Magic Barrier is an area spell. Even when on the Mahora campus where Evangeline's magical power is restricted the spell is still quite powerful and can even block physical attacks. However, Asuna, who has magic-canceling abilities, was able to break it without a problem. It was also pearced by Fate's Stone Lance spell and broken by an attack by Sestsuna during the Martial Arts Tournament.

Ice Burst

A large amount of ice forms in the air and blasts anybody who is near.

Crystallized Earth

A spell that calls forth large icicles from the ground, freezing feet to the ground and is especially effective if used against enemies who can't fly. The spell is invoked by uttering, "Come, spirits of ice, spread forth into the air! Tundra and glacier in the realm of white night! Crystallized Earth!".

The End of the World

A spell with a 150 square-foot area of effect that lowers the temperature of everything within its range to absolute-zero after which enemies can either be broken to bits, or kept frozen to immobilize them. Needless to say, the spell is rather powerful. It is invoked by uttering, "Heed the pact and serve me, Oh Queen of Ice. Come forth, unending darkness, eternal glacier! Bring death to all that has life, eternal rest! The End of The World!"

Blizzard of Darkness

As the name implies, the spell summons a dark and powerful blizzard. Evangeline used this spell once against Negi to counter his related Jupiter's Storm of Thunder spell. The spell is invoked by uttering, "Come, spirits of ice and darkness! Oh snowstorm which blows with darkness! Blizzard of Darkness!"

Hammer of the Ice God

An attack using a giant ball of ice. The idea behind the spell is rather simple but makes up for it with the size of the ball that is made. It's not a very high level spell and Evangeline can use it as a chant-less one.

Executioner's Sword

An attack that summons a sword made of ice. Evangeline uses this spell as a chant-less spell so it is thought that it may not be one of her strongest. Nevertheless, it is quite deadly.

Fate's Magic

Breath of Stone

A smoke-like spell used by Fate that can turn people to stone. It is invoked by uttering,

"Small eight-legged lizard king, and master of the evil eye. Steal time with your poisonous breath!"

Evil Eye of Petrifaction

A beam spell that turns anything in it's way to stone. It is invoked by uttering, "Small eight-legged lizard king, and master of the evil eye. Let the disastrous light emit from my hand!"

Stone Lance

An attack spell that summons a mass of jagged rocks. This spell is a compilation of two types of magic and can be used to shatter an opponent's magical barrier.

Chao's Magic

Blazing Heat in the Sky

An old Greek spell that is capable of immense heat and can incinerate almost anything within its range. It is related to Evangeline's End of the World spell and is of comparable power. It wouldn't be difficult for the Shinso vampire to cast but it was very difficult for the magicless Chao and she had to use future technology to force her body to cast the spell, leaving her in great pain. The spell is invoked by uttering, "Heed the pact and serve me, O Tyrant of Flame. Come, flame of purification, fiery broadsword. Fire and brimstone surging forth, Sodom was burning, turning the sinners into the dust of death. Blazing Heat In The Sky!"

The Magic of Others

Black Clothing Nocturne

A spell used by Takane D. Goodman. This spell draws on the power of shadows a summons a demon that fuses with the caster making her faster, stronger, and better suited to close combat. Takane becomes powerful to the point that she doesn't require a partner.

Red Blaze

A spell used by Mei and Chao, it is a fire-based spell that destroyed enemies with intense heat. It can be used underwater or in a vacuum. The spell is invoked by uttering, "Ever-burning fire of purification, Lord of Destruction and Sign of Rebirth, gather in my hand and strike my enemy! Red Blaze!"

Imprisoning Wind

A wind spell used by Kataragi that traps enemies within a cyclone of wind. The wind is dangerously powerful and the barrier cannot be forced apart. The spell is invoked by uttering, "Surging summer tempest. Imprison them in the wind!"

Restraint of Flowing Water

A spell used by Megumi that can bind people with water from a spout. Oxygen is infused with the water making it possible for people to breathe while trapped, but the oxygen can also be cut off for a fatal effect.

Restraint of Fire

A spell used by Mei can entangle enemies in a spiral of fire. The fire isn't actually capable of burning those it captures, but it feels as hot as a sauna. Escaping it requires some magical know-how and if escape is impossible, it will begin to hinder blood-circulation and may be fatal.

One Thousand Bolts of Lightning

A spell used by Nagi that can unleash an unlimited number of lightning bolts onto his enemies.

Other Magic

Fire Lamp

The first spell learned in magic school where a small fire is made on the end of a staff. It may seem a little boring at first, but it can be used underwater and experienced casters can make the flame quite large. Negi says that people have been using fire for a long time and points out that it is thought to have an important meaning as the foundation of modern society. Misora used this spell during the school festival to navigate Chao's underground labyrinth.

Fortune-Telling Magic

Magic that can predict the future. Along with Fire Lamp, it is a basic spell and one of the first ones learned. Predictions are more precise with how experienced the magic user is and this type of magic can be used with the Cassiopeia to make it more accurate.

Magic for Moving Objects

Small objects can be moved or manipulated by spiritual force. This is also a spell that is learned early on and higher skill means that smaller objects can be controlled more accurately.

Healing Spell, Cooler

The first healing spell that is learned. This spell can heal light injuries, but not serious ones or illness. Konoka is practicing with this spell.

Flying Magic

Magic that can be used for flying on a staff or broom and doesn't require an incantation. This spell can be used to carry people other than the caster but in this case the staff or broom may become overburdened and unstable. While flying there is a special force field that keeps riders from falling off and also serves as a veil that makes the riders invisible to those on the ground.

Memory Eraser

When Asuna first learned about Negi's being a mage he tried to use magic to erase her memory but accidentally ended up blowing her clothing off instead. Negi figured that he simply made a mistake, but that was actually the result of Asuna's magic-cancelling nature. Gandolfini also tried to use this spell on Chao to keep her from revealing the existence of magic.

The incantation for this spell is unknown.

Medicine Making Magic

This is magic that Negi used to make a love potion for Asuna, he later discovered that this is illegal.

Breast Enlargement Magic

A spell that can make an air bubble by borrowing spiritual power from the air element.

Negi used this spell on Asuna to create air bubbles around her breasts to make them look larger but the air bubble eventually popped. Later, Anya and Nodoka performed the same spell on themselves with the same result. The spell in invoked by embarrassingly uttering, "Air, air, make the chest bigger!"

Object Manipulation

A spell used to animate objects. The spell is invoked by uttering, "Dance brushes!"

Three-day Genius Spell

It looked as though Negi's class was going to do poorly on the final examinations so he thought he would use this spell on some select students to help raise the class average. The only problem is that after the three-day limit is up, the person who had the spell cast on them looses what little intelligence they had to begin with for one month. He was going to use it on Asuna but she stopped him before he could cast it but it wouldn't have made sense to do so anyway since it was four days before the exam at that point.

Self-Sealing Spell

Negi used this spell to seal his own magic before his class took the final examination. It looked as though they were doomed to fail and he was tempted to help them so he decided to use this spell to resist the urge. Originally this spell was used on enemies and one black bar appears on the wrist of the person inflicted with the spell for each day their magic is locked.

Refreshment Spell

A basic spell that can be used to cure fatigue that requires flower petals as a catalyst to boost effectiveness. The spell in invoked by uttering, "The fragrance of a flower, a wind that will fill my friends with energy, vitality and health! Recovery!"

Staff Calling Spell

This spell can be used to call a staff back to the owner if it is dropped, lost, or needed in the case of an emergency. The spell range of effect is unknown but it is thought that the owner must know where the staff is located before he or she can call it.

Voice Alteration Spell

This can be used to change one's own voice, and possibly that of others as well.

Dream Viewing Spell

This spell can be used to peer into the dreams of those who are asleep. This spell is invoked by uttering, "Mave, queen of dreams. Open the door to the dream world." It is also possible to see the intentions of others by use of a pactio card.

Attendance Hell

This is a strange spell that Nagi used to restrict Evangeline to the Mahora Academy campus while also dampening her magical powers. Nagi cast this spell to get her off of his back under the pretext that she needed compulsory education and would be released after she had finshed. This spell is supposed to keep young kids from skipping class, but Nagi's version is in an endless loop which means Evangeline must start from the beginning of secondary school after she has already finished it, but part of the spell is that this doesn't arouse the suspicions of others.

Evangeline has currently been going to class for 15 years and she will be finishing secondary school for the sixth time. It's currently not known where Nagi or the book he used to cast the spell is so there is the possibility she may never be free of the curse.

During the field trip to Kyoto, Konoemon was able to send Evangeline as backup only by fooling the spirits that enforced the curse by writing a note every five seconds stating that she was away from the school on for study. This was obviously only a temporary solution but it served the purpose in the end.

Distance Spell

Working like a barrier, this spell that can be used to keep people a certain distance away from each other. This spell doesn't work on ghosts or magic users.

Concentration Breaker

This is an ermine spell Chamo uses to break the concentration of magic users.

Thought Synchronization

Magic used for synchronizing thoughts with another person. The translation of language is automatic if both people speak different ones.

Wind Protection

A spell used by Negi and Yue to protect clothing from wind

magic. Wind can cause a lot of problems for skirts.

Wind, Protect Us

A spell used by Negi that is capable of wrapping people in wind to protect them from falls.

Genjutsu

Genjutsu is a type of illusionary magic. Evangeline used to use this type of magic often to make herself appear older but, because of the Attendance Hell curse, she could only use it during the power outage, when she went to Kyoto, and inside her villa where her power isn't restricted. Genjutsu is thought to be rather high-level magic. However, there are age-deceiving pills for those of us without super great magic skills. Evangeline also used genjutsu on Setsuna during the Martial Arts Tournament to try to disorient her.

Mitsuru's daughter is also able to use genjutsu and did so to attack those who were trying to rescue Negi from the party, but Yue was able to see through it. She uses illusions of beasts and Takamichi.

Magic to destroy illusionary worlds

This is magic to destroy illusions. Yue leaned about this type of magic in hopes of tearing down the illusion of Mitsuru's daughter's World Picture. She didn't have enough power to cast the spell on her own though so she used Asuan's artifact for assistance. Yue didn't believe that it was an illusion at first, so genjutsu must also have the effect of hiding its own existence, no matter how unreal a situation may seem.

Breeze

This is one of the beginner spells. It makes it possible to blow over light objects.

Glint

This is one of the beginner spells. It's a fire-elemental spell and creates a strong flash that can temporarily blind an enemy.

Delay Spells

A way of delaying a spell from the time the chant is complete to the time it is actually cast from anywhere to a few seconds to upwards of a minute. This can be used to a tactical advantage in battle allowing a spell caster to time combinations or to chant when they are able to defend from attacks. During the fieldtrip to Kyoto, Negi used a time delay of over 20 seconds.

Magic Gates

This is a high level spell used for teleportation and during the school trip Evangeline used it to arrive at the Kansai Jujutsu Association's headquarters. It is unknown if this spell requires an incantation.

Fate uses water as a median

for this spell and Evangeline uses shadows.

Magical Items

Love Potion / Medicine

Negi was able to make a love potion and Chamo ordered some love chocolate off of the Maho Net. Negi made the love potion for Asuna to use on Taka-michi so that he would return her feelings. He didn't have confidence in his own magic though so she made him drink it instead, instantly attracting all of the girls in the school except for Asuna because of her magic-canceling nature. The effects of the potion only lasted for a short time though.

The kind of love medicine that Chamo ordered was in the shape of bite-sized chocolate that was to make the person who ate it fall in love with the next person they saw. The effects of this medicine last for half a day. Asuna had eaten one earlier and confidentially found herself being drawn to Negi but, again, because of her magic canceling ability it is unlikely that this was the result of the medicine. Shortly afterward Konoka ate some and fell in love with Setsuna, prompting Asuna to throw the chocolate out.

Book of Melchizedek

Before class 2-A's final exams, Negi and a handful of his students sought after this legendary book that is supposed to give its reader extensive knowledge. The book is deep under Library Island and was being protected by a golem. They were eventually able to steal the book from the golem but had to abandon it upon entering the elevator to the ground level because it was too heavy. Later it was learned that Konoemon had possession of the book and had planned this whole scenario.

Magic Letters

Letters that are capable of playing the voice and displaying an image of their sender. These kinds of letters have been used between Negi and Nekane, as well as Chao when she sent one to Asuna declaring victory for the "Negi Party".

Evangeline's Resort

This is an item that Evangeline made herself and has let Negi use it for his training. It looks like a miniature tower-shaped building on some sand and enclosed in a glass jar, but one can enter it by standing in a special location outside of it. The resort is equipped with a spa and a pool and time flows differently inside it with one day being the equivalent of one hour outside of it. It has been said that time travel cannot be carried out with magic, but this is a place where time is sped up.

Inside the resort, the temperature is controlled to be like

that of an everlasting summer and it does change from day to nighttime. The resort also allows Evangeline to tap into her true power allowing Chacha Zero to move about on her own accord.

Evangeline created an illusion of her resort for the fight with Setsuna at the Mahora Martial Tournament. Takamichi also trained in her resort for many years, which is why he looks older than he actually should be.

Red Candy / Blue Candy, Age-Deceiving Pills

This is candy that Chamo ordered off of Maho Net which casts an illusionary spell on the person who eats it with the red candy making that person look older and the blue one making the person look younger. The pills are able to alter the age within a range of 5-7 years. As an illusion, the user doesn't go through any physical changes, but it is necessary to change clothing for some reason. There is a time limit for this spell.

Each candy is expensive at over $15 per piece but it is popular and has been used by a variety of people including Chachamaru, Mana, Konoka, Setsuna, Kotaro, and Chisame.

Originally, Negi used one to look older so that Asuna could practice building the courage to ask Takamichi on a date by practicing on Negi. He was only able become five years older though. He has also used them to escaped from the media after the trournament, to go on a date with Ako, and to gain entry into the tournament, but the rules were changed in the end anyway.

When somebody has a pill to look older it's not a perfect representation of how they will actually turn out, but rather a reflection of how they want to look. Negi wanted to grow up to be like his father, and Konoka wanted to have a nice body.

When fleeing from the media, Negi was able to use a pill and change into new clothing while in the Ferris wheel, leading some to speculate that he must either carry these things with him or be able to summon them to his location.

Anti-inanimate Object Magic

The magic used on everybody at the school during the last day of the school festival. This was during the fight with Chao's robot army and it was used by the magic using teachers. It was able to stop all things that are not living such as golems and robots. This was also used against Evangeline to keep her from using her puppets. In recent years, a new type has been developed.

Keyword Index

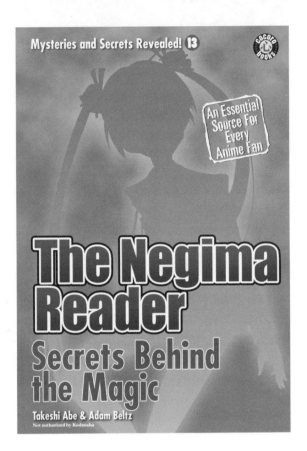